THE LAST OUT

MATTHEW SULLIVAN

WET BANDIT

For Elmer and Charlotte

1

I t wasn't very long ago that I was ready to give up on almost everything: school, friendships, and sometimes even life. If not for a seemingly minor decision that ended up rerouting the entire course of my life—I just might have. The decision, which I made so quickly that it bordered on being a spontaneous reaction, was to tell Derek Whitney to eff off.

It all happened shortly after I left my first-period history class. Derek had stopped me in the hall to tell me he liked my new haircut. "Cool haircut" were his actual words. He said it with a slight smirk, which led me to believe that he wasn't serious. And that's when I dropped it on him like a hammer.

To be clear, I didn't go with the friendly phonetic form. Nope, I opted for the full four-letter version—or seven, if you count "off" too—in all its vulgar glory.

Not the nicest thing to do, I know. It's even worse when you take into account that from the first day of second grade until about six weeks before the beginning of that school year—our sophomore year at Fort Myers Academy—Derek had been my best friend.

In my defense, I hadn't intended to unload my aggression on Derek. My harsh words were really meant for the universe, with which I was in an ongoing war. And Derek, well, he just happened to get in the way. But not for long. Just as fast as I dropped my f-bomb, I dipped my shoulder and slipped past him.

Unfazed, Derek turned and followed me down the packed, locker-lined hallway. "I wasn't making a joke," he insisted, weaving through the crowd and quickly catching back up to me. "I seriously think it looks good."

I still couldn't tell if he was being honest or if he was just kidding, but I was leaning toward the latter. Regardless, I didn't really care. "I bet," I said, not slowing down or turning to acknowledge him. "You said the same thing last week about my boots."

"I know. And I really like them too," Derek said, albeit much less convincingly.

He'd shown his cards. He was lying about the boots, which meant he had to be lying about my hair. The metal buckles on my weathered and two-sizes-too-big combat boots rattled even louder as I picked up my pace.

Derek matched me stride for stride. "Okay. Fine," he conceded. "I admit it. I'm not a fan of the boots. They're totally weird, and I don't really get them. They also look seriously uncomfortable. But I do think your hair looks good. It's cool. Different, but cool."

Different was an understatement. The buzzed sides and jet-black mop on top—which perfectly matched my boots, jeans, and t-shirt in both tone and attitude—were so diametrically opposed to every other hairstyle I'd previously sported that I still didn't recognize my reflection. Part of the reason I'd refused to believe that Derek liked my haircut, or really anything about my new look, was because I still didn't know how I felt about it. All I knew was that there was one person who loved all of it; her name was Grace Kwon. I also knew that she was waiting for me at my locker and that Derek was not only slowing me down but also likely to follow me all the way there if I didn't get rid of him.

I stopped on a dime and whipped around to Derek.

He jumped back and threw up his hands. "I wasn't kidding, seriously," he insisted. "It looks really good on you."

"I don't even care anymore," I said. "But I have a feeling that's not what you actually wanted to tell me. So, what do you really want?"

"Oh, yeah," he said, averting his eyes. He started to fidget around, kicking his feet. "I, uh—I mean my, um—"

"Dude!" I said and threw my hands up. "I don't have all day."

"Sorry. It's just ... my parents wanted to invite you over to dinner tomorrow. That's all."

"Seriously? Your parents do?"

"Yeah. I mean, I want you to come too, but they suggested it. To make up for the last time and everything."

The last time I had dinner at Derek's house, it hadn't exactly gone well. In fact, it was the beginning of the end of my friendship with Derek.

The dinner went down just a few days after my parents gave me "the talk" and told me they were separating. I was supposed to spend the night at Derek's too, but I didn't even make it to dessert. While the Whitneys laughed and smiled and had their usual, polite dinner conversation about how great their days had been, I stayed mostly silent, opting to just nod my head when spoken to. It wasn't fun, but it was fine. At least it was until about ten minutes into the meal, when I asked for the peas and was promptly corrected by Mr. Whitney.

"You mean please, right?" he said.

"Yeah, peas," I mumbled, not hearing him correctly.

"Yes. You would like the peas, but you forgot to say *please* pass the peas."

Instead of apologizing and kindly asking for the peas again—please included—I just glared at Mr. Whitney.

"*Please* pass the peas," he repeated and forced a smile.

"No!" I snapped. "Just give me the goddamn peas, or don't give me the peas."

Mr. Whitney's eyes went wide. The rest of the family just froze, their mouths agape.

After a few seconds of awkward silence, I shook my head and said, "Forget it. I don't want the peas."

"No, no, no," said Mrs. Whitney. "It's all right. Everything is all right. You can have the peas." She spoke so fast that she needed to take a deep breath before continuing, "Clifford, please pass Jordan the peas. Give him the peas."

"Of course," Mr. Whitney said, nodding excitedly as he offered the bowl. "Have as many peas as you'd like."

I took the bowl, purposely withholding any thanks or show of gratitude, and then dumped a heaping spoonful onto my plate. Half of the tiny green veggies tumbled over the edge of my plate and onto the table, with half those continuing onto the floor.

"Jeez, Jordan," Derek said and then bent over to clean up my mess. "Don't take it out on us."

"It?" I asked, turning my anger on him. "What do you mean?"

"I, uh, I don't know," he stuttered.

"No. I think you do. What's 'it'?" I demanded.

"You know." Derek swallowed hard. "Your stuff."

"My stuff?"

"Yeah, the stuff that's going on with your parents, man."

"Screw you." I chucked my napkin onto my plate and shot up from the table.

"Come on," Derek pleaded, getting up as well. "I didn't mean anything by it. Where are you going?"

"I'm going back to my broken home." I started for the door and then stopped, turning back to the wannabe Cleavers and their quaint family dinner that I'd ruined. "You guys act all perfect, like you have this perfect, happy family and life. But no one is this perfect. No one!" And with that, I stormed out of the house.

To his credit, Derek had called every day for a few weeks, even though I never answered or returned the calls or even listened to his voicemails. Eventually, his calls stopped. The cord was cut, with Derek and the rest of our little group of friends.

When school started back up, Derek and I would have our awkward interactions every couple of days, passing each other in the halls and stuff like that, but that was about it. His dinner invite was the closest thing to a conversation that we'd had in months.

"So, what do you think?" Derek said, eager for an answer. "You can also spend the night. I just got the new *Call of Duty*, and it's super badass."

I could see how badly he wanted me to say yes. Part of me wanted to say yes too, to just go back to the way things had always been. "I don't know," I said.

"Come on. It will be a lot better. I promise. My parents have really loosened up a ton. I don't even have to say please for anything anymore. I still do, out of habit and all, but I don't really have to." His grin grew, like we were sharing an inside joke.

But the joke was more of a reminder of that night and only brought back the lingering animosity that I still held close. I could just imagine how much his parents would judge me now, and all the things they'd say since I'd "gone goth." With my rage reignited and combined with the added agitation of Derek refusing to just leave me alone and let me get to my locker and Grace, I decided to end the conversation once and for all.

"That's really great to hear," I said. "Lucky you. Do me a favor, though ..." That's when I told him to tell his parents to "please" eff off. I flashed two flexed middle fingers as substitutes for exclamation points and then turned and walked away.

Unlike the first time, Derek didn't follow me. He just stood there, stunned, for a few seconds before screaming at me to eff off. "All I ever did was try to help you," he continued. "But you don't want help. You just want to be an asshole."

I didn't look back or say anything. I just continued to pick up speed as I headed down the hall, ignoring the stares from the rest of the students who had stopped whatever they were doing to watch me.

2

I didn't give my run-in with Derek a second thought as I hurried down the hall. All I could think about was Grace and making sure that my strides never got so long that my speed walking could be confused for running. Vice-Principal Goldenberg was always lurking and seemed to get off on giving out detention to anyone who broke his imaginary speed limit.

By the time I finally rounded the corner to the small alcove where my locker was, most of the other students had already switched out their things and headed to their next classes. There were just a few stragglers and no sign of Grace.

Convinced my distraction with Derek had caused me to miss her visit, I flung my backpack the fifteen feet to my locker and then plodded the rest of the way. I was so pissed off that I messed up my locker combo three times. After finally entering the correct combo, I yanked the door open, switched out the books in my backpack, and then slammed the door shut.

"Easy," Grace said, wincing and covering her ears with her palms. "What did that locker ever do to you?" She lowered her hands and let out a big bubbly grin. The light-hearted joker that she was, she'd snuck up behind my opened locker door while I was busy brooding. But now that she was there, smiling at me, all my angst instantly washed away.

As surly as I was when left to my own thoughts, I couldn't help but adopt, as if by osmosis, the exact opposite temperament around Grace. This was especially true when she was happy, which was pretty much all the time. All it took was seeing her glowing face, and I'd instantly forget about everything wrong in my life and the world. That is, until my nerves set in.

Grace and I had only been officially "dating" for three days and unofficially for about two weeks, which meant that I'd yet to advance past the stage of getting catastrophically anxious every time we started a new conversation. I would've given anything to have just butterflies in my stomach. The creatures in my belly were closer to rabid pterodactyls, assuming pterodactyls could get rabies. With each whip of their wings, it felt like my chest was about to explode. That was the first response, followed by a total loss of sensation in my hands and feet.

I've heard someone say that conversations in the early stages of a relationship are like flights: takeoffs and landings are the most likely times of crashing. I couldn't agree more. To keep myself from saying something wrong while our talks were still on the tarmac, I would stay quiet and let Grace take the controls of the conversation until my nerves calmed down a little.

Grace flicked my bangs to the side and smiled even wider. "They're already looking better than yesterday," she said. "In another month or two, they'll be perfect."

"I think they're perfect now," I said, smiling back. "You did a great job."

"Well, aren't you just the sweetest?"

You are, I thought, but it never came close to crossing my lips. We were nowhere near the cruising altitude required for something so cheesy. Instead, I just kept grinning.

"I was thinking there's just one more thing that would really help tie your look together." She retrieved an eyeliner pen from her purse and held it up. "You can say no, but I think it'd look really, really good."

She was so damn cute trying to sell me on it, that there was no way I could say no. "Sure, I'll try it."

Grace chewed on her lower lip with her teeth while she concentrated on applying the eyeliner. I desperately wanted to be the one biting her lip, kissing her. However, going for what would have been our first in-public kiss and our fourth kiss overall, would have required a lot more confidence than I was capable of summoning. Instead, I just stared at her lips, fantasizing. Every couple of seconds, she'd catch me and remind me to look up.

"Done!" she said after a few more strokes. "I think it looks great, but what do you think? Do you like it?" She held up a tiny clamshell mirror for me to see. "If you don't, it washes off super easy."

Much like my hair, I wasn't sure how I felt. But knowing that she liked it, meant that I liked or was at least willing to roll with it. "It looks great," I said.

I'd had a crush on Grace since the spring of eighth grade, but we hadn't shared more than a few words until three weeks earlier, on the first day of school. By luck, they put us in the same Chemistry class. By an even greater stroke of luck, I happened to wear a black Polo shirt to school that day. It was another one of those seemingly minor decisions that completely changed everything. When it came time to find lab partners for the semester, Grace picked me and told me that "black looked great on me."

Predictably, I rushed home after school that day and dug through my closet and dresser, scouring for anything with even a hint of black. With only a meager haul, I rounded up all my cash, rode my bike to the nearby TJ Maxx, and loaded up on as many black t-shirts and pairs of jeans as I could afford.

A week later, during our first unofficial date, Grace helped me pick out my combat boots at the local Salvation Army, and I retired my neon blue New Balances, which didn't fit the new me.

Before making the switch, I'd always assumed that all goths were the same. But Grace informed me that they weren't and that there were even subcultures within the tiny Gothic community at our school, which really just comprised Grace and four other kids, or five if you counted me. Grace described herself as a perky goth. While she still wore a lot of black clothes and makeup, she also mixed in a decent amount of pink and purple. She also didn't have the same disgruntled demeanor that I had; she was always upbeat. Grace chose to be goth because she liked to be different. She also enjoyed shocking people, especially her tiger mom. When I started dressing goth, I swear my parents didn't even notice. They were too busy with their own issues. But Grace noticed, and that was all that mattered.

"Changing gears," she said, grabbing my hands and shaking them enthusiastically. "I have some mega huge news."

"What?" I said, sharing in her excitement.

"My brother came through."

"That's awesome!" I said, forcing a smile because I had no idea what she was talking about. "And it's about damn time that he did what he hadn't done."

Grace giggled. "You don't know what I'm talking about, do you?"

"Not a clue," I admitted. I knew she had a brother, Michael, who was a junior at the University of Miami, at least he was supposed to be, but that was pretty much all I knew.

"I thought I told you last night, but I must've just been thinking it," Grace said and then explained that she had tried to get her brother to connect her with his old pot dealer the year before; however, being the occasionally responsible older brother, he'd refused, claiming that she was too young and that he'd only make the connection after she was older than he'd been when he first tried weed. Apparently, that magical age was fifteen years and two hundred and twelve days. It was a threshold that Grace had unknowingly passed a week earlier but had only become aware of after she'd returned home from cutting my hair and called her brother to check on her status. With the hookup from Michael, she called his "guy" and scored a dime bag.

"I was going to call you to tell you about it," she said, "but I wanted to save it for when I saw you."

"I can see why," I said. "That's definitely in-person news. That's, you know, radical. If people still say that. Maybe they do. I mean, I just did." Truthfully, I was only excited because Grace was excited. I wished I hadn't been so excited and had also stopped talking after I'd said "news."

"I know," Grace said, beaming. "My brother said it's amazing stuff too. So, I was thinking we could all meet out back by the loading dock during lunch and try it."

"Wait. Like today? Like school-day lunch?" I said, trying to conceal my shock and doing a terrible job of it.

"Yeah, school-day lunch," Grace said and grinned as if I was just making a joke. "Like in a few hours."

"Well, shouldn't we—" I was cut off by the bell. Startled, it took me a second to recollect my thoughts. I cautiously continued, "I mean, shouldn't we, maybe, like, I don't know wait until after school and just go to someone's house?"

"Everyone has plans. Same for the weekend."

"I don't know. The loading dock during school? It seems a little risky."

"It's not. My brother said he went there every day when he was at school here. All his friends did too. He said no one ever got busted there because no one ever goes back there. Just the janitor and garbage trucks. He said it's pretty much the safest place there is." She held her smile while she waited for my response.

"Yeah, uh, that might be true, but ..." I said each word with a hesitant stutter that knocked Grace's grin down a notch as it left my lips. By the time I'd finished, the corners of her mouth had already begun sloping downward. I quickly backtracked. "I mean, I want to. I just don't want to waste my high on Mr. Salner's Chemistry class, that's all. Plus, we could do some damage with the Bunsen burners."

Grace studied my eyes, which I'm sure said: I'm full of it and really don't want to do this. After a few seconds, she averted her gaze, glancing down at her feet. "It's okay," she sighed. "We don't have to do it."

Grace's disappointment was as obvious as the black dye that still stained my scalp. As much as I didn't want to go, I didn't have a choice. While a midday smoke session was probably the second-to-last thing that I wanted to do, upsetting Grace held the top spot by a long shot.

I lifted her chin with my finger, looked her in the eyes, and with all the fake confidence I could muster said, "I'm in."

Grace bought it. Her smile returned, and so did mine. While her's likely lasted until we saw each other again, mine only lasted until the end of the hallway, where we split up to head to our second-period classes. That's when the reality of what I'd signed up for settled in.

3

W hile I'd been able to convince Grace that I was down with her plan, the truth was that I was scared shitless. Even though I'd made steps in my growth as a goth, I had yet to graduate to "rebelling against the authoritarian hierarchy," which was how Grace's friends described some of their activities. I'd mostly maintained my straitlaced status, albeit in a new and less-than-straitlaced package.

So, for the next three hours, as the second hand dragged across the classroom clock face, I nervously watched every tedious tick. With each passing minute, my insides twisted into more and more tiny knots. If I would've had an abdominal MRI, I'm pretty sure my stomach would've looked like a crowded circus tent of balloon animals.

My belly of balloon animals got bigger and bigger until it was popped by my Spanish teacher, Señor Newman, who caught me staring at the clock with ten minutes left in class. "Señor Lewis," he said and snapped his fingers. "Atención, por favor."

I almost jumped out of my seat. "Oh, sorry," I said and turned my head toward the front of the room.

"En Español, por favor."

"Si. Uh. Lo siento."

Mr. Newman smiled, nodded, and went back to describing diphthongs. After I regained a little of my composure, I went back to obsessing over the waning seconds before my date with Mary Jane, counting in my head while keeping my gaze on the chalkboard to maintain the appearance of paying "atención."

NINE MINUTES LATER, the bell rang, and everyone shuffled out of the classroom. Just about everyone in the school headed to the cafeteria or at least in that direction. I plodded against the flow of traffic, toward the exit on the far side of the school that led to the loading dock.

I made two turns, a right and then a left. With each turn, the student traffic thinned out more and more. I passed by the entrance to the band room just as Derek was exiting with his trumpet case in tow. He stopped and shot me a nasty look, but he didn't say anything. I didn't either. I just continued down the hall and made a third turn, another right. After that, I was alone, with only twenty feet of vacant hall to go until the exit.

Grace and her friends were nowhere to be seen. I wasn't sure if I was the first one there or the last, but I was the only one. My mind immediately began to search for a way out, any passable excuse: I was the first one there and thought everyone bailed ... I'd assumed we were meeting in the cafeteria first ... I was stopped by a teacher or hall monitor. I—

A firm slap on my back jolted me from my brainstorming. I whipped around to find Billy Green towering over me from behind. Already tall on his own, the four-inch rubber soles on his black leather boots made him a shade over 6' 8" and almost a full foot taller than me. As usual, a long black trench coat covered his lanky frame, his hair was slicked back and matted down, and his eyes were hidden behind the tiny, circular lenses of his wire-framed sunglasses.

"This is your last chance," he said, staring at the door. "After this, there's no turning back."

"Wait. What?" I stuttered then swallowed hard.

"Seriously?" Billy groaned. "You gotta be kidding me. It's only a line from one of the biggest scenes in *The Matrix*. It's right before Morpheus offers Neo the red pill or the blue pill."

"Oh. Yeah. I mean, I remember that part. Just not all of it."

"You continue to disappoint me, Hair Jordan," Billy said and shook his head.

Realistically, remembering the movie quote still wouldn't have endeared me that much to Billy, or "Neo" as the self-proclaimed world's biggest *Matrix Trilogy* authority preferred to be called. He was the self-appointed leader of Grace's motley crew of friends and not the biggest fan of yours truly. He had two reasons for not liking me: one, because he had a crush on Grace, and two, because he thought (or knew) I was a total poser. That's what he called me for the first week I started hanging out with them, until he came up with the Hair Jordan nickname, a play on Michael Jordan and my initial reluctance to dye my hair dark.

Billy lifted his shades, studied my head, and then lowered his glasses back onto the bridge of his nose. "Although, it looks like I'm gonna need to come up with a new nickname for you," he said. "Maybe Jordache for your dark ass jeans."

Much like the dye on my scalp gave away its recentness, the fresh darkness of my clothes, which not even Woolite detergent could guarantee, was like a leftover sales tag that couldn't be removed. Meanwhile, all of Billy's clothes, and even his sunglasses, had a slightly faded touch of gray from years of wear and sun, which he wore like a badge of authenticity.

"Whatever makes you happy, *Billy*," I said, stressing the Billy part. I knew it got under his skin, much more than his nicknames bothered me, and I saved it for special moments when I really wanted to dig at him.

Billy snorted derisively. "It's Neo, dick," he said and then forcefully flipped the collar of his trench coat and strode toward the door.

Now that Billy had seen me, my excuses went out the window. Like Neo, there was no turning back. I took a deep breath and then followed Billy outside.

The rest of the gang was already gathered by the small U-shaped alcove and hiding behind a couple of dumpsters. A cell phone rested on the nearby dumpster lid, playing some song by The Cure from its tiny speakers.

When Grace spotted me, she ran up and gave me the biggest hug she'd ever given me. "I was starting to get worried that you weren't gonna come," she said.

"Yeah, well, I practically had to drag him," Billy scoffed.

"That's not true at all," I said, coughing as I inhaled a whiff of the rotten dumpster fumes.

Grace retrieved the goods from her pocket—a tiny Ziploc bag the size of the top of my thumb. For such a small bag, it produced a more pungent, albeit piney, stench than even the dumpsters. Grace handed the bag to Billy, who immediately went to work on rolling a joint while the rest of us baked in the scalding September sun.

"Ugh, I can't wait to get the hell out of Florida," said

Midnight, a dedicated vampire goth whose real name was Gloria Estevez, as she held up her hand to shade herself. She only wore long flowing dresses and parted her black hair down the middle like the mom from *The Addams Family*. She was rarely without her clear Nalgene bottle, which was always filled with a dark red liquid. If anyone ever asked what was in it, she'd grin and say blood, but according to Grace, it was just Hawaiian Punch. By far, her most frequent sources of frustration were the sun and her Cuban complexion, both of which prevented her from being as pale as she wanted to be. Midnight shook her head at the bright ball of fire that hung in the sky like a navel orange, the official fruit of Florida, and groaned, "This state is the worst."

"I concur completely," said Absinthe, a steampunk goth whose actual first name I didn't know, but I was pretty sure it was Joshua. Most of the other kids in school just called him Fat Slash. He'd moved to the area in the middle of my freshman year, and he showed up to school looking like a huskier version of the guitarist from Guns 'N Roses. He even sported the same curly black hair and stovepipe hat. He removed his hat and wiped his sweaty brow with the frilly sleeve of his Victorian-era military jacket. "I've lived across much of this green earth, or at least much of this country, and fully support your sentiment. The only thing worse than the sun is the people."

"Well," Grace said, chipper as always, "I've never been there, but you should totally check out Alaska when you graduate. I think you'd love it."

"That assumes that I would or could love anything other than the metallic taste of blood," Midnight said.

"I think you would and totally could. I have a cousin who lives in Fairbanks, and she said there are weeks in the winter where they only get a couple of hours of sun. And even when it's up, it's more like dusk than it is like this."

"There's just one problem with that plan," said Betty, the last member of the crew. Betty was a gothabilly—an interesting mixture of goth and rockabilly—whose real name was Betty. She'd been previously preoccupied with the Sharpie tattoo of Elvis that she was adding to her left forearm to match the Marilyn Monroe etching she'd doodled on her right forearm. She capped her pen, slipped it into the pocket of her polka dot poodle skirt, and looked up and continued, "For every day of darkness she'd get in the winter, there's also a full day of nothing but sun in the summer."

"Well, yeah," Grace said. "But at least the sun is weaker in the summer there."

"Still. It's a whole day of sun."

"Yeah," Midnight agreed. "Weak or not, I don't think there's any way that I could survive that."

"Tierra del Fuego," I blurted out.

Everyone, except for Billy, who was completely focused on his task at hand, turned to me, surprised that I'd offered anything. I didn't usually contribute much to the group discussions. I mostly stayed on the outskirts and occasionally nodded, so they knew I wasn't dead.

"Land of fire," Midnight said, translating the name. "I like it already. Tell me more."

"It's the southernmost tip of mainland South America," I said. "Since it's the Southern Hemisphere, the seasons are flipped. So, you could live in Alaska during our winter and live down there during theirs. That way, you maximize your night time."

Midnight considered my suggestion for a second, judging me

as much as she was my idea. She cracked a smile. "I like the idea." She turned to Grace. "And I'm really starting to like your boyfriend."

"Me too," Grace said. "He's so great."

"Just peachy," Betty added.

"Thanks," I said, cracking a tiny and short-lived smirk of my own.

"Enough of this Jordache lovefest," Billy said, having finished rolling the joint. "I don't have all day. I got a super important video game tournament after school, and I still need to finalize my tactical strategy."

"Jordache?" Absinthe asked, not catching the reference.

"That's Hair Jordan's new nickname. I just came up with it."

"That's not how it works," Midnight said. "Everyone gets to pick their name."

"Yeah, well, he can figure it out later. Till then, he's Jordache. Now, who has the fire?"

Absinthe reached into the breast pocket of his jacket and produced a vintage Zippo lighter. He flipped the lid and sparked the flint in one fluid motion, and then extended the flame to the joint, which Billy held between his thin, clamped lips.

"To deny our own impulses," Billy said out of the corner of his mouth and then inhaled, the tip of the joint turning as bright as the sun. He withdrew the joint from his lips and closed his eyes, holding in his breath. He slowly exhaled a stream of gray smoke, opened his eyes, and then smiled as he continued, "Is to deny the very thing that makes us human." Billy took another, shorter puff and then grinned at Grace, impressed. "Wow. Your brother really came through. This is some red-pill, down-the-rabbit-hole shit."

Grace beamed and rubbed my arm excitedly. I forced a weak and twitchy smile.

Absinthe accepted the joint from Billy, inhaled for a surprisingly long time given how weak his lungs had seemed in the gym class we shared, and then exhaled an equally impressive cloud of smoke that blanketed the whole crew like a winter's fog. As he let out the last plume, he began to cough so hard that I thought he might strain a muscle. "That is phenomenal stuff," he said in between coughs. "Top notch. I wouldn't be surprised if it was laced."

"Don't be a dumbass," Billy said. "No one laces weed. That's an idiotic myth and terrible business. Then they'd just be giving drugs away for free."

"Not if they charged you for it."

"Did they charge you?" Billy asked Grace.

She shrugged. "I don't know. I don't think so."

"Well, there you go."

"Whatever," Absinthe said. He nodded to Grace. "I know you don't smoke." And then turned to me and offered the joint. "Care to partake?"

I was too busy processing Absinthe's previous statement to answer. While Grace and I had never talked about it specifically, I'd always heard that all the goth kids "smoked weed" and "did drugs." With Grace being part of the crew, plus the fact she'd gone out of her way to procure it, I'd just assumed that she would definitely "partake."

My confusion must have been apparent. When I turned to Grace, she immediately offered an explanation before I could even get a word out. "I've tried it before," she said, "but it didn't really do anything for me. I thought that maybe it'd help you though. You know, take your mind off everything, since it seems to work for my brother and his anxiety."

It all made sense. That was why she'd been so excited at my locker and why she was so disappointed when I was reluctant to join—she'd done it all for me. Without realizing it, I had clearly vented about my parents way more than I thought the night before. My complaining was at least bad enough for Grace to decide that she had to call her brother and try to do something to help pick me up.

Any feelings of nervousness that I'd previously had disappeared entirely. I smiled back at Grace and said, "Thanks." I took the joint from Absinthe, pinching it with my fingers.

"Gentle," Absinthe said.

"Sorry." I loosened my grip. I glanced at the joint, then at Grace, who was beyond giddy, and then back to the joint.

"It's not gonna smoke itself," Billy said. "It's one of the laws of physics. Actually, it's Willie Nelson's first law. A joint at rest will stay at rest."

"However," Absinthe said, "a laced joint abides by its own set of physical laws."

"Dude, it's not laced," Billy said, annoyed.

"You can honestly tell me you aren't getting any tracers?"

"Yeah, I can."

I don't know if it was the music, which was still whining over the cell phone speakers, Billy and Absinthe's arguing over whether the weed was laced, or the rest of our laughter over their ridiculously heated argument, but none of us heard Vice-Principal Goldenberg as he exited the school and crashed our little smoking session. It wasn't until he shouted, "What the heck is going on back here?" that we realized we were all busted.

4

N one of us even tried to run. There was no point. We would've merely been delaying the inevitable. After all, you can't really claim "mistaken identity" when there aren't any other kids in the entire school that fit even a quarter of your profile.

Vice-Principal Goldenberg escorted us to Principal Forte's office, leading us by the cafeteria on our way. Everyone inside the cafeteria giggled and pointed as we marched past the glass wall. I spotted Derek, our eyes locked for a split second before he jerked his head, averting his gaze. I immediately knew that he'd ratted us out to Vice-Principal Goldenberg.

Once we made it to the main office, Vice-Principal Goldenberg had us sit as far apart as possible and instructed us not to say a word while he reported the news to his boss. Principal Forte's secretary, Mrs. Bower, shot us the evil eye and made sure that we sat in silence.

All things considered, I stayed relatively calm throughout the whole ordeal. There were no pterodactyls, or even butterflies, in my belly. I wasn't the slightest bit worried about my parents being upset when they found out. I was almost excited to see how they would react. I smirked to myself and then turned to Grace, expecting to find a similar look of satisfaction on her face, but what I saw was the opposite—she was afraid.

That took an eraser to all my excitement. I wanted to hug Grace and tell her not to worry, anything that might make her feel better. I opened my mouth, but before I could even get a word out, Mrs. Bower stopped me with a stern shush. I kept my mouth shut and tried to comfort Grace with my eyes, but she couldn't even look at me.

A minute later, Principal Forte finished consulting with Vice-Principal Goldenberg. He let us know how disappointed he was and said that he would speak to us individually and intended to "get to the bottom of this."

I immediately offered to go first. Billy tried to undercut me, most likely assuming that I was going to snitch or pin it on him. But that was never part of my plan. I stuck to the plan I'd come up with while watching Grace's nerves get the best of her. As soon as Principal Forte closed the door to his office, I told him it was all my fault—it was my idea and my marijuana.

I know the others were shocked when they had their meetings with Principal Forte. Instead of getting the grilling they expected, they were just asked to corroborate my version of events. They happily did, and they couldn't hide their disbelief and relief as they exited Principal Forte's office with grins on their faces, their wide eyes immediately turning to me like spotlights.

The only person who didn't smile was Grace. I could tell she was relieved, but she wasn't happy. She looked at me and mouthed, "Thanks." Mrs. Bower was watching me closely, so all

I could do was give Grace a quick smile. It got me a smile back, which made everything seem better, if only for that moment.

After we'd all met with Principal Forte, Mrs. Bower called our parents to pick us up. Absinthe's father, a former Army officer who acted like he never left the service, was the first to arrive. After a brief meeting with Principal Forte, he dragged Absinthe away by the ear while informing him he'd finally "punched his ticket to military school." As serious as his father sounded, I couldn't imagine Absinthe surviving military school, much less doing a push-up.

Midnight, Billy, and Betty's mothers came next, in that order. Each of their exits weren't remotely as eventful as Absinthe's. Just dirty looks and headshakes, and then they each followed their peeved parents out of the office. Although, I did get a little enjoyment out of watching Billy whine to his mother about how he couldn't miss his video game tournament.

I figured my mom would fall somewhere between Absinthe's dad and everyone else's moms on the anger scale. I was wrong. When she finally showed up, almost a half-hour later, you would've thought she was there for a regular parent-teacher conference. Unlike all the parents before her, she didn't wear any emotions on the sleeves of her pantsuit. She just nodded at me, a simple acknowledgment of my presence, and then continued into Principal Forte's office and shut the door.

Grace and I shared a look. "That was weird, right?" she mouthed.

"My mom's weird," I mouthed back. "That was normal."

That got a little smile out of Grace and got me a glare from Mrs. Bower.

"No talking," Mrs. Bower reminded me as she shook her head and tapped a pencil on her desk.

A minute later, Principal Forte's door opened. My mom thanked him for his time and then nodded at me again. "All right. Let's go," she said calmly, and then started for the office exit without checking to confirm that I'd listened.

Grace and I shared one last look, and she mouthed, "I'll text you."

"Good luck," I mouthed back and then followed my mom, purposely lagging.

As I made my way to the school exit, I spotted Grace's mom charging toward the glass doors. I instantly knew why Grace had been so nervous; her mom looked even more furious than all the previous parents combined. Knowing what they say about first impressions, I held off on introducing myself to Mrs. Kwon. Instead, I shielded my face as I held the door for her. She just charged through without a thank you or any kind of acknowledgment.

I sighed and continued toward the parking lot. My mom was nowhere in sight, but her SUV was easy to find. It was plastered with so many stickers and banners advertising her re-election campaign for State Attorney that the vehicle looked like it belonged on a NASCAR track. I took my time walking to the car. When I got there, I was about to go for shotgun, but then thought better of it. I opened the back door, tossed my bag on the seat, and climbed in.

My mom had both of her hands tightly wrapped around the wheel as she stared straight ahead. "This is the last thing I need to be dealing with," she said through gritted teeth. She was angry, after all. She'd only kept her composure for political purposes and waited until we were in private to let her true feelings be known. "You realize I need to be re-elected to keep my job, right? Do you want me to lose? Is that what you were hoping would come of this?" I wasn't planning on responding to any of her questions, but before I could, she snapped, "Don't answer that!" She cranked the keys in the ignition and then pulled out of the parking lot.

As we drove down the stoplight-lined street, my mom wrestled with her inherent need to obey all traffic laws and her increasing desire to take her aggression out on the road. I swear the engine made the closest sound to a rev that I'd ever heard in all my times riding with her. Her hand even came within a few inches of smacking the horn before she pulled it back.

"Of all people," my mom fumed as she stopped at a red light and turned to me, "you should know not to say anything until you have an attorney present."

I kept quiet. I didn't care what my mom thought. Plus, I was more concerned with how Grace was faring with her mother and Principal Forte. I waited until the light turned green and my mom's gaze returned to the road, and then I retrieved my cell phone from my pocket. I typed a text to Grace, *How'd it go?* and hit send.

My mom continued her ranting, "I bet I know where you got the marijuana from too. You stole it from your father, didn't you? I've always told him you'd eventually find his little stash one day and take some. It isn't brain surgery."

Saying something wasn't "brain surgery" was my mom's way of getting under my dad's skin. Understandably, the cliché is like nails on a chalkboard to anyone who, like my dad, is actually a neurosurgeon. Leading up to their separation, I'd anticipated something bad was about to happen with my parents, because my mom's frequency of comparing menial things to brain surgery kept steadily, if not exponentially, increasing, to the point that she started saying it even when my dad wasn't around.

"That's where you got it, right?" my mom demanded as she stopped at another light. She turned to me again, expecting an answer; however, what she found was me staring at my phone, waiting for an answer of my own from Grace. "What are you doing?"

I was about to say "nothing" when my phone buzzed. Grace had responded. I scanned the words as fast as I could. *Not good. My mom went ape. She said I can't see you anymore.*

I wasn't too surprised about that. I'd expected her mom to react, or overreact, in a similar fashion. What I hadn't expected was what happened next. I was in the middle of texting her back *LOL* when the phone buzzed again. She beat me to it. Her text was short and to the point, just one word.

Sorry.

Sorry? I didn't understand why she was sorry. Any confusion I had about what she meant was answered with the next text, which came a few seconds later.

It's over.

I couldn't believe it. She was really following her mother's orders and breaking up with me. I wanted to text her back, to say the right words to convince her not to do this, but my thoughts were spinning through my head like a tornado, and I couldn't think of a damn thing to say other than begging her not to listen to her mother. Before I could even get the chance to write that, my mom reached back and snatched the phone right from my hands.

"What the hell are you doing?" I said, angry and confused and still struggling to process Grace's obedient acceptance of her mother's wishes.

"I'm taking your phone away," my mom said matter-of-factly and then shoved my phone into her pocket.

"Give it back! I need it."

"What you need is an attitude adjustment, not a phone. A phone is a privilege. And so is your freedom. Which means both can be taken away. You're grounded, from all things, indefinitely. And if you think you're just going to sit at home, by yourself, and text and watch movies all day, you're in for a rude awakening."

Little did she know, I'd just had the rudest awakening I could ever receive, and there was nothing she or anyone else could do to hurt me. It was over. Everything was already over.

My mom hit the call button on the Bluetooth speaker clipped to her sun visor and said, "Call Robert work." The call connected and the administrator at my dad's hospital answered and said that my dad was just about to go into surgery. My mom assured the administrator that her call was an emergency and instructed her to put the call through.

My parents went at it while my mind replayed reading Grace's text over and over like some sick and twisted TiVo that had gotten a glitch and was stuck on a loop. The only thing that saved me was my mom yelling, "Did you hear your father?"

"What?" I said.

"Just promise me one thing, Jordan," my dad said. "Promise that you'll stay away from the harder stuff, especially ecstasy, because that really does damage your brain."

"Whatever," I groaned. I couldn't have cared less about my dad's advice or what either of my parents wanted to tell me about drugs, life, or really anything. I would have gladly taken the brain damage if it took the pain I was feeling and the memory of Grace's text message with it.

"Don't talk to your father like that," my mom snapped with a look to match.

"Sorry, I learned it from you," I said smugly, a nod to the old anti-drug commercials.

"That's not funny. Not funny at all. I've had more than enough from you."

"It's fine," my dad said, breaking us up over the tiny speaker. "For now, I'll take it. All right, I need to get into surgery. Jordan, I love you, and we can talk about all of this on Saturday when you come over."

"Whoa! Wait a second!" my mom shouted, cutting my dad off before he could finish his goodbye. "He's suspended for the rest of the week. I need to drop him off with you."

"That won't work. I'm operating for the next eight hours and then all day tomorrow."

"Yeah, and I have to be in court and then have a fundraiser tonight that I—"

"Don't worry, Georgia," my dad said, cutting her off this time. "I'm sure you'll figure it out. No one works harder or smarter than you. Besides, it isn't brain surgery." I heard a faint chuckle from my dad as he used my mom's line on her and then hung up.

My mom stewed. "Great," she said. "Just great. Now, what am I going to do with you?" And then, her scowl morphed into a sick, mischievous grin. "I know exactly where to take you," she said, her smirk growing as she took pleasure in her plan.

5

Punta Gorda was only twenty miles from my house, but it felt like a different world. The town was incorporated in 1900, and the running joke was that it was also the birth-year of most of the residents. According to the most recent census, nearly half of the population was over the age of 65, thanks to the many sprawling retirement communities.

My mom banked a right and pulled into Punta Gorda Gardens, the biggest retirement community in town, passing a sign at the entrance that exclaimed, "Punta Gorda Gardens: If Only Your Life Before Punta Gorda Was This Great." Life on the outside appeared to live up to their slogan, with the palm trees, manicured grounds, and courts for all the recreational activities that you have to be really old to enjoy, like bocce, croquet, and shuffleboard. It was straight out of a brochure. The only thing missing from this picture-perfect package was the smiling cross-section of seniors, all having the best time ever. However, they couldn't be found on the Punta Gorda Gardens grounds or anywhere inside the halls, because they didn't exist. All the residents we encountered from the parking lot to the front desk and down the residence hall were indifferent at best. It was just how I'd remembered it.

While I'd only been to Punta Gorda Gardens once before, a little over a year earlier, I knew exactly where my mom was taking me. I'd known since she'd blown past the turn to our house and continued to the highway. Just three flights up in the main elevator and then a right and a left, and we'd be at my grandpa's apartment, or condo, or assisted living home, or whatever they called it.

When we arrived at the apartment—number 348, which I distinctly remembered because Grandpa Kalb had argued with the leasing agent when they tried to put him in a different room —my mom knocked on the door. A few seconds passed without a response. A worried look crossed my mom's face. She knocked again, even harder the second time.

The answer was almost immediate.

"Jesus Christ, I heard you the first time," an irate Grandpa Kalb mumbled in his thick New Jersey accent. "Just hold your damn horses." I could hear him fumble with the locks on the door as he continued to complain, "I don't know what the hell you want any—"

Grandpa Kalb stopped mid-sentence as he finished opening the door and discovered us standing in the hall. He froze, like Han Solo in carbonite, a petulant look plastered on his face.

"Hi, Dad," my mom said. "Can we come in?"

Her words hung in the air for a second before Grandpa Kalb finally snapped out of his fog. When he did, it was like a switch flipped, and he put on the most overcompensating and fake, at least to me, enthusiasm. "What kind of question is that?" he hollered, spreading his arms wide and welcoming. "Of course, my dear! Come in! Come in!"

We entered the apartment, which consisted of a tiny kitchen, a living room, and a door that led to the bedroom. The place looked almost exactly like it had when Grandpa Kalb moved in, save for the two felt New York Yankees pennants mounted on the wall above the tiny 20-inch TV that was playing *SportsCenter*. Other than the pennants, the place was void of any personal touches. It was downright depressing, even to me, which given what I was going through and my overall mindset at the time, really says a lot about how depressing it was.

I shuffled over to the alcove next to the entrance, averting my eyes and doing my best to go unnoticed. I pretended to scan the place while honing my ears on my mom and grandpa so I could eavesdrop on their conversation. Not only did I want to hear what my mom had to say but my mind kept drifting back to Grace and concentrating on their conversation was the only way to distract it, the only way to keep me from having a total breakdown.

"I didn't expect to see you," Grandpa Kalb said.

"I know," my mom said. "I'm sorry for the lack of notice. And I'm even more sorry that it's been so long."

"No apologies needed. It hasn't even been that long. I've barely been here a year."

"God," my mom sighed. "I thought it was less than that. Now I feel even worse."

"Stop it."

"I've been meaning to come by. It's just that I've been so busy with work and campaigning and everything else and—"

"Hey," Grandpa Kalb said and held his hand up to stop my mom. "I'm the last person you need to explain anything to. You got a lot going on. You're working your tail off, as you should, and I couldn't be prouder of you."

Feeling like I was safe enough in the background, I snuck a peek of my mom out of the corner of my eye as she smiled. Grandpa Kalb smiled back; however, his eyes told a different story than the rest of his face. They welled up, just the tiniest bit in the inner creases.

My mom noticed it too. "Is everything all right?" she asked.

"It's better than all right. I'm great!" Grandpa Kalb wiped the corners of his eyes with his thumb and forefinger and then let loose an even toothier grin. "I'm just so happy to see you."

"Seriously?"

"Yeah. Should I not be?"

"That's not what I'm saying. You promise you're all right?"

"Cross my heart. You don't gotta worry about this guy."

My mom kept sizing up her father, trying to get a better read. She was used to breaking lying witnesses on the stand and was damn good at it. I'd never been able to get even the smallest fib past her. "There's something," she said. "I can tell."

"It's nothing," Grandpa Kalb said, trying to brush it off while proving that my mom was correct in her questioning.

"What is?"

"It doesn't even have to do with me."

"What doesn't?"

Grandpa Kalb sighed, finally giving in. "A friend of mine had a stroke this morning."

"Oh, my god. I'm so sorry."

"It's fine. It is what it is. Stuff like that happens all the time here. Pretty much every day ending in Y."

"Dad?" my mom said, concerned by his tone.

Grandpa Kalb turned away and changed topics. "Can I make you a sandwich or anything else to eat? You're looking a little skinny," he said as he made his way to the fridge and then opened the door. "I have ham and turkey."

My mom didn't respond. She just stood there, trying to decide if she should keep pushing or just let it go. It was an even battle between her need to rush back to the campaign trail and her worry for her father. Like with so many other things, the campaign won out in the end. "I'll take that as a compliment," she said, "but I actually can't stay long or at all, really."

"Oh," Grandpa Kalb said, letting his disappointment show for a split second. He gently closed the fridge door.

"I have a huge favor to ask," my mom said, clasping her hands and smiling nervously.

"Sure. Whatever you need."

"So ... your wonderful grandson was just suspended from school. Robert is in surgery all day, I'm swamped with campaign events, and the last thing I want is for Jordan to be at home by himself, getting into even more trouble."

"So, you need me to whip him into shape and lay down the law?"

"If you could just watch him, that would be fine," my mom said with a grin. "I can pick him up around nine tonight or whenever works best for you."

"Hmmm," Grandpa Kalb said and rubbed his chin, pretending to think it over and doing a bad job of pretending. "I'm just messing around. Of course, I'll watch my grandson! When are you planning on dropping him off?"

My mom chuckled at the cheesy joke. I rolled my eyes at the both of them.

"Oh!" Grandpa Kalb said, feigning astonishment, which was even worse than his previous acting job. "That's him? I didn't recognize him with the dark hair and makeup and everything. I thought he was just some convict you were transporting to lock up."

"He's just going through a phase," my mom said and then turned to me.

I quickly averted my eyes, only connecting with her gaze for a split second.

"Ah," Grandpa Kalb said. "So that's what they're calling it these days? When I was his age, we didn't have time to go through 'phases.' We were too busy working ... our second jobs." His delivery was like a bad imitation of Rodney Dangerfield. I half expected him to say that he "got no respect" next.

"Kids these days," my mom said, "don't even have first jobs."

"And people wonder why this country is going to hell in a handbasket. As if it isn't obvious. It starts with the work ethic."

"I don't want to cut you off," my mom said with a smile as she put her hand on Grandpa Kalb's arm, "but before you get too riled up, I really do need to get going."

"Of course," Grandpa Kalb said as he nodded a little too emphatically, trying to show that he was okay with it. "I don't want to hold you up with my angry old-man rants."

"Once the election is over, we can start having weekly dinners like we talked about. And I expect to—no, I want to hear all of your angry old-man rants."

"You do realize I got a lot of them, right? I've been saving them up, especially about the Yankees. I don't know if you've been following them, but they're pissing the damn season away."

"I honestly haven't had time."

"I know, I know. Well, you haven't missed much anyway. We're down eight games to the goddamn Sox. Our 13-year streak of making the playoffs is about to end at the same time as the stadium. But at least we won last night, and we still got a puncher's chance."

"That's good. That's all we need. And thank you so much for helping me."

"Anything for you, sweetie."

My mom nodded at me. "You listen to your grandpa." She turned back to Grandpa Kalb. "And don't let him watch any of his TV shows or anything like that."

"Don't worry. I won't," Grandpa Kalb said.

"You're the best. I love you."

"I love you more."

My mom grinned and hugged Grandpa Kalb.

After they let go of each other, Grandpa Kalb gave her a kiss on the forehead and then drew a small cross with his thumb where he'd kissed. "Now get the heck out of here and go win that election."

My mom turned to me. I assumed she was looking for a hug. Instead, I shot her a look that let her know it wasn't happening. She shook her head and threw her hands up in defeat. "I'm not even going to bother," she said and then headed out of the apartment.

Just as soon as my mom was out the door, all the fake hope and happiness disappeared from Grandpa Kalb. He glared at me, looking me up and down like a corrections officer checking in a new inmate. "What the hell happened to you?" he said. "You used to be such a sweet kid."

I kept my mouth shut, gritting my teeth.

It didn't stop Grandpa Kalb, he just continued, "Thank god your grandmother doesn't have to see what you've turned into. It'd break her heart." He started to circle me, getting even closer.

"What'd they pop you for, anyway? Wait. Don't tell me." He leaned in, took a big whiff, and then smirked. "Marijuana. The Devil's lettuce. Just as I thought. You got the look of a weed smoker. I don't know any personally, but you sure fit all the stereotypes."

I could see where this was going and decided I'd had enough. "Is this how it's gonna be?" I said. "We're really gonna do this all day? I just stand here while you chew me out."

"Of course not," Grandpa Kalb said. "Everyone knows addicts like you have sticky fingers. I don't trust you around my things. Hell, I already saw you casing out the place before. You probably already got a plan to pawn my TV to support your habit."

"I'm not an addict," I said. "And I definitely don't have a habit. Even if I did, no one would buy your crappy TV."

"Ah-ha! So you *were* checking out the place. Unfortunately for you, we won't be here for much longer. Just let me turn off the TV, so I don't waste any electricity."

"Where are we going?" I asked. I had no clue what he had planned and couldn't help but feel a little unnerved. For all I knew, he was going to try to take me to some military school like Absinthe's dad.

"Don't you worry about it," Grandpa Kalb said as he grabbed the remote control, which was resting on the kitchen counter, and turned off the TV. He retrieved his apartment keys from the hook next to the entrance and then opened the door. "After you."

6

O f all the activities Punta Gorda Gardens offered, the worst, at least from a spectator's standpoint, and it wasn't even close, had to be their midday karaoke. I would've much rather watched a bunch of octogenarians try to play shuffleboard or even sunbathe nude than poorly sing a bunch of terrible songs that I'd never even heard before. But, that's exactly where I ended up, sitting in the back of the cafeteria with my grandpa.

On the tiny stage at the front of the room, some guy named Art, who sported inch-thick glasses and a mismatched and slightly off-center toupee, belted—which is the best way to describe his singing since it felt like my ears were getting a spanking—some song about flying to the moon and playing with the stars or something like that.

I did my best to tune out as much of the racket as possible but had little to no luck. The only thing that came close to quieting all the clangor were thoughts of Grace, which were even harder on my heart than Art's singing was on my ears. So, singing it was. I shook my head, groaned, and slunk into my uncomfortable vinyl chair.

Grandpa Kalb glanced at me and snorted derisively. "Oh, I'm so sorry this isn't your cup of tea."

"It's more like a cup of pee," I said. "I'd rather go back to your place and get yelled at."

"Too bad. Like I said before, I don't trust you around my things."

"Well, there's gotta be somewhere else we can go. I'm almost ready for someone to fly me to the moon on a one-way trip, just so I don't have to listen to this crap."

"Crap?" Grandpa Kalb said, making a face as if he had written the song and I was insulting him personally. "This isn't crap. This is the Chairman of the Board."

"Which board, Lehman Brothers?" I had no idea what Lehman Brothers was, but I'd seen a recent news story about them declaring bankruptcy, so it seemed fitting, topical, and likely to annoy my grandpa, which was my main goal.

"Ha. Ha. Hilarious. That's not what I meant. It's Frank Sinatra."

"More like Stank Sinatra," I said. "A heaping, stinking pile of crap."

This riled up the old man even more. "Frank Sinatra was one of the greatest singers of all time!" He huffed and puffed, releasing the rest of his steam. After a moment, he let out a tiny self-satisfied smirk, clearly amused by what he was about to say. "You know, this might come as a surprise to you, but back in my day, you could be a successful musician and not dress like a weirdo."

Little did he know, he couldn't hurt me with his jokes. I was too numb. "That doesn't surprise me," I said and then flashed a grin of my own. "What surprises me is that you could be successful by singing such crappy music."

Grandpa Kalb bit the corner of his lip and shook his head. "Whatever," he said, looking away, "I'm done arguing with you."

"You're giving up already? That was a lot quicker than I expected. I figured it would take you longer to realize you can't win an argument about how much Sinatra sucks since it's so obvious that he does." My grin grew as I glanced at Grandpa Kalb. I was confident I'd get a rise out of him, but he didn't even flinch. He just kept looking straight ahead, and I slumped back into my seat.

We sat in silence for about a minute while Art switched from lyrics involving lunar travel to having his heart filled with song, and then Grandpa Kalb broke his silence. "For the record," he said, no longer angry and much closer to contrite than anything else, "I want to be here a lot less than you. And I'm not just talking about this cafeteria. I'm talking about here in general."

"I have a hard time believing that," I said. "You were the one who chose to move down here to this place."

"Yeah, well," Grandpa Kalb said, his voice growing heavy and gaining weight with every word, "that was only after a lot of things I didn't choose."

I knew he was talking about my grandma's death. She'd died from stomach cancer when I was twelve. Since they had lived in New Jersey and we'd only seen them once or twice a year, I didn't have as many memories of my grandma as I probably should have; however, all the ones I did have were fond ones. I hadn't forgotten the green plastic suitcase that she always brought, which my dad would have to lug from my grandparents' car and complain about how heavy it was, whenever they drove down to visit. I'd never forgotten how wide she smiled when she saw me or how tight she squeezed me when she said goodbye. I'd never forgotten how she always smelled like fresh apple pie, even if she wasn't baking one, or how she loved to do laundry, which she called "doin' a warsh" in her Baltimore accent. All those memories and more flooded my mind until Grandpa Kalb regained his composure.

"But even so," Grandpa Kalb continued, "there's a strong chance that the last game in the history of Yankee Stadium is gonna be played this Sunday, and I should be on my way there right now, instead of babysitting your keister." He let out a deep sigh. "That game was the only thing I've had to look forward to in the past three years. I already had great tickets and everything. Ten rows up on the third-base line. The best place to watch a game at Yankee Stadium."

"Then go," I said. "You're an adult. Nothing's stopping you."

"Ha!" Grandpa Kalb howled, genuinely amused. "Spoken like a true teenager. When you're young, you think you can do anything when you're older. Then, you get old and realize there's still so much that you can't do. And then you get even older, and that's when you lose the ability to do all the things that you actually could do. Remember my friend who had the stroke, the one I told your mother about?"

"Yeah," I said and nodded.

"Well, he was gonna drive. I was on my way to his place this morning. He'd just called and said he was ready to go when"— Grandpa Kalb whistled: his sound effect for the stroke—"it hit him. Now he's in a coma. Odds are he'll never come out of it."

"That sucks."

"It sure does. It sucks big time. And that's life for you."

"Yeah," I agreed, for my own reasons and for his as well. I couldn't help but feel bad for this man that I'd never met and also for my grandpa. His friend's stroke had stirred some feeling deep inside him. I gave him a second to himself before pointing out the most obvious solution to his problem. "Why don't you just drive by yourself?"

"It was his car, and I don't have a license."

"So? Neither do I. All I have is my permit. But that didn't stop me from taking my dad's car for a drive once last summer. Just don't get pulled over, and you'll be fine."

"You realize I'm gonna have to tell your parents about that, right?"

"Like I care. It's their fault anyway. They were too busy working and fighting to help me practice for my behind the wheel."

Grandpa Kalb stared at me. "You really are a piece of work, aren't you?"

"I'll take that as a compliment."

"It wasn't one."

"I'm still taking it as one. And you should take your friend's car and go to the game."

Grandpa Kalb shook his head and sighed. "It's not just that I don't have my license," he said as he turned and gazed off. "They took it away for good reason. I lost most of my peripheral vision, thanks to the glaucoma."

I peered into the corner of his eyes, searching for any visible signs of deterioration, as if I knew what I should be looking for and there was something to be found. His eyes were a little bloodshot but otherwise seemed normal.

Grandpa Kalb continued, "If I got behind the wheel, I'd not

only be a risk to myself but also to everyone else on the road." I waved my hand side-to-side, my crude vision test to determine if his eyes reacted to the movement of my hand. They didn't; however, his whole head did, whipping in my direction. "What the hell are you doing?" he barked, scowling at me.

I yanked my hand back. "Nothing. I thought you lost your peripheral vision?"

"I did, but I can still feel a goddamn breeze."

"Oh," I said with an apologetic smirk and then quickly changed topics. "Well, why don't you just fly? It's better than driving anyway."

Grandpa Kalb glared at me for a second before letting my little science experiment slide. "I'm not allowed to," he said. "The doctor's got me on a new heart medication, and I can't fly on it. I also can't take the bus or train, because there's too much bacteria on public transportation. That pretty much eliminates pretty much all my options."

I tried to come up with another way to get to New York, but the only alternative I could come up with was my main mode of transportation, riding a bike, and that didn't seem very practical, especially with his strict time frame. "I guess you really are stuck here," I said.

"Yep," Grandpa Kalb said and then bit his lip and nodded slowly, "In more ways than one." He sighed, slumped down in his seat, matching my posture, and then stared out the window and off into the distance.

Meanwhile, my good friend Art had finished his little number and was offering the microphone to anyone in the disinterested audience. I half-contemplated going for it and screaming a song from one of the death metal bands that I'd heard Absinthe rave about. The looks of shock on the rest of the audiences' faces would've been priceless. Of course, I knew that there was also a good chance it might cause a few coronaries too, so I held off. None of the other audience members took Art up on his offer either.

"In that case," Art said slyly, "I'll just have to give you a little more magic from Ol' Blue Eyes. I don't know if you heard the news, but I'm about to start spreading it." He hit a few buttons on the shoddy karaoke machine, but nothing happened. He hit a couple more. Still nothing. "Just give me a second or two, and then the news is really gonna start spreading."

Without Art to distract me, I zoned out, my thoughts drifting back to Grace and her text messages. Not just the "It's over" but the "Sorry" too. Was she really sorry? If she was, it sure didn't seem like it. It seemed like she didn't even try to put up a fight. She just immediately followed her mother's orders. It seemed like she was content letting our relationship end just as it was getting started. Worst of all, it seemed like she didn't care about hearing my rebuttal, what I had to say about the matter.

Without my phone, there was nothing I could say. There was nothing I could do. The only thing I had going for me was gone. I was staring down possible expulsion, potentially a new school, definitely no girlfriend, and, on top of it all, Art's raspy voice, which broke my train of thought as his music finally started playing.

Art crooned, or at least attempted to, about spreading the news and leaving for New York, New York. I wanted to scream, "Do it!" But I kept quiet, the lyrics strangely worming their way into my brain. My foot began to tap to the beat. I was buying into the song. Well, not the song as much as the message. I needed to spread some news of my own. I needed to get the hell out of Punta Gorda Gardens and South Florida in general. I needed to get away from my parents and Grace and her parents and everything else. Screw the authoritarian hierarchy; it was time to rebel! It was time to run away, and no better place to do it than New York. In Florida, I'd get found in a flash. But, in New York, with eight million people going about their business, I could disappear forever.

I shot up in my chair and grabbed my grandpa's thigh.

Grandpa Kalb practically jumped out of his seat. "What the hell?"

"I'll drive," I said.

"What are you talking about?" He looked at me like I was crazy. In his defense, I'm sure I had a crazy look in my eyes.

"I'll drive us to New York. Let's do it. Let's go. Let's get the hell out of here."

"Are you serious?"

"Yeah," I said, shaking my head emphatically. "I'm one hundred percent serious."

"Then you are insane. And, as a rule, I never get in an automobile with anyone with loose screws."

"You don't make any sense," I said, confused that he wasn't immediately on board with my plan. "I thought you wanted to go to the game."

"I do. But I wouldn't let you drive me to the 7-Eleven down the street for a Slurpee, much less all the way to New York City."

"Why not? I can do it. Besides, it's your only option."

"No. It doesn't even count as an option. You don't have a license."

"I have my permit and can drive with anyone over eighteen,

which you're pretty safely above. Plus, I'll have my license in a few months, assuming I pass. That's pretty close."

"Close only counts in horseshoes and hand grenades. Besides, we're not talking about some little joyride in your dad's BMW. It's a twelve-hundred-mile trip, with at least twenty hours of driving."

"That's only five hours a day. That's nothing. Besides, I lied a little when I said that I took my dad's car out once last summer. I've actually taken it out at least ten times." That was a lie, and so was my first claim that I'd even taken out my father's car at all. But I wanted to sell my grandpa on the idea that we could make the trip. "I can handle the drive."

"Be honest with me, are you a sociopath or something?"

"Of course not."

"You know, that's exactly what a sociopath would say."

"It's also what someone who isn't a sociopath would say, so it's kind of a stupid question, don't you think?"

"Yeah, I guess so." He stopped, contemplating for a moment. I wasn't sure if he was chewing on the circular logic of his sociopath question or on my proposition to drive us to New York. And then, his face tightened, and I knew it was the latter. "But it doesn't matter. You could've taken his car a hundred times. That still wouldn't mean you could actually make the drive. At least not in my book."

"What if I told you his car was a stick?"

Grandpa Kalb tilted his head and arched an eyebrow. "It is?"

I nodded. It was another lie. It was my dad's old car that had been a stick. I knew that would mean something to my grandpa. I had remembered a conversation that he had with my parents about it. While I didn't recall the specifics, I remembered my grandpa being impressed by that.

"You know your grandmother drove for almost fifty years and was still never able to drive a stick shift?" he said, shaking his head gently and grinning as he reminisced. "I tried to show her at least a dozen times, but she just couldn't work the clutch without stalling out."

"I didn't know that," I said; however, him saying that jogged my memory of the conversation, which included some of that information. "But, like I said, I can drive."

I could see the wheels in Grandpa Kalb's mind turning. His solidified stance was softening; he was moving onto the fence. I knew that whatever I said next had to be good, to help push him over to the right side, my side. But, before I could come up with the perfect closing line to my pitch, he just shook his head and said, "No. It's not happening. End of discussion."

"But—"

"I said end of discussion. You know what end means, right? That means there's no more discussion."

"Fine," I griped. Like any good angst-ridden teen, if I wasn't going to get my way, I was damn sure determined to get in a few parting blows. "I guess you don't really want to get out of here like you said you did. You'd rather just be stuck here and complain about it. Whatever. I didn't want to go to some stupid, boring baseball game anyway."

While I thought Grandpa Kalb had taken it personally when I ripped on his boy Sinatra, that was nothing compared to his reaction to me calling baseball stupid and boring. His face lit up like a fuse that set off an explosion in his body and resulted in a spastic fit of disbelief. "Excuse me?" he said, regaining control of his limbs. "Baseball is a lot of things, but boring ain't one of them. It's the greatest game there is, and the greatest game there ever was."

"Yeah, right," I said, exhausting every ounce of sarcasm in my body, "just like that Sinatra guy was the greatest singer ever?"

"Exactly," he exclaimed, willfully disregarding that I made my comments in jest. "You know why baseball is so great?"

"It isn't great. It sucks, and I was obviously being sarcastic about Sinatra."

Grandpa Kalb ignored me again and continued, "I'll tell you what makes baseball better than any other sport, it's that you can't just sit on a lead and run out the clock. To win, you gotta throw the ball over the goddamn plate and give the other guy his chance. Earl Weaver said something like that, and it's true. Every team gets their nine innings, their 27 outs. Then, and only then, does the game end."

Grandpa Kalb sat with his words for a second, and so did I since I didn't have anything witty or biting to say.

After a moment, Grandpa Kalb started back up, but in a much softer and serious tone, "Life would be a lot better if it was more like baseball. If we all got our 27 outs, and we all knew the count. Instead, we're all playing on our own clock, with no clue when in the hell or how it's gonna run out."

A smirk slipped across my lips as I prepared to deliver my final blow. My coup de grâce, which Grandpa Kalb had perfectly teed up. "Well, the good news is that at least you get to stay by yourself in a great place like this until it does."

My shot connected hard, much harder than I had even expected it would. Grandpa Kalb looked like all the life had been sucked out of him, which sucked all the enjoyment out of me. Thoughts of guilt popped into my mind like browser ads. One little click and they unleashed malware that overtook my mental hard drive.

But, just when I was about to apologize, Grandpa Kalb's tortured expression evaporated and was replaced by one of sheer determination. "Screw it," he said. "I changed my mind. Let's get the hell out of here."

7

We hurried back to Grandpa Kalb's apartment, only slowing down momentarily when we passed by an open room door or the occasional orderly wandering the hall. When we made it back to the apartment, Grandpa Kalb went right to his bedroom to pack a few things for the trip while I waited near the door like he'd instructed me to do. Even though we were on our way out, he was still worried about his stupid TV.

A minute into my wait, my growling stomach reminded me that I hadn't had lunch. I remembered the sandwich that Grandpa Kalb had offered my mom and decided to make one for myself. I opened the fridge and found that it was almost bare. My mom was lucky that she hadn't taken Grandpa Kalb up on the turkey because there wasn't any. All he had was a little ham, which was one of my least favorite lunch meats. The only things I liked less on a sandwich were bologna and chunk light tuna. However, at that point, I was so hungry that I would've eaten them all together. I snagged the last piece of bread, which happened to be the end piece, another least favorite of mine, folded it like a taco, and slapped on a couple of slices of ham and a pickle spear.

I was down to the last couple of bites when Grandpa Kalb returned from the bedroom carrying the green plastic suitcase from my childhood memories. He watched me chomp on the ham sandwich taco and nodded excessively. "Great! I hope you enjoy that. Don't even worry about asking or anything."

I stopped, mid-bite. "I would've asked, but you were in the other room."

"Oh. So that's how it works these days? Manners and common courtesy just go out the window when someone leaves the room? Well, don't let me get in your way. Help yourself to anything else."

"I don't think I could. It's not like you have a lot of food."

"I don't? How would you know? Did you go through all the cupboards? You wanna go through my underwear drawer too?"

"I'll pass. And I only went through the fridge."

"Well, that's reassuring."

I sighed. We hadn't even left the apartment and our trip was already getting off to a painful start. I decided that it was in the best interest of my own sanity to be the bigger person and smooth things over. "You're right," I said. "I still should've asked. I'm sorry for going through your fridge and taking your food."

"Thank you," Grandpa Kalb said, genuinely surprised and appreciative that I'd apologized. "If you're still hungry, I might be able to find some more stuff for you to eat."

"I am. And that would be great."

As he dug through the mostly empty fridge, Grandpa Kalb explained that he hadn't gone shopping the past week, since he'd been planning for his trip. "That's the kind of stuff you have to take into consideration when you're older," he added, moving on to the adjacent pantry. "With what they're charging for milk these days, you can't afford to let a gallon, or even half a gallon, go bad. You'll go bankrupt doing that."

"I'll make sure to remember that," I said, pretending to be interested.

"All right," Grandpa Kalb said as he set the rest of the ham, a half a bag of carrots, an apple, a mostly empty jar of peanut butter, and half a sleeve of Ritz crackers on the counter, "this is all I got left. Have at it."

"Thanks."

"Can't let it go to waste," he said and rolled up the last quarter-pound of deli meat and chomped it down. "There are few things more satisfying than completely cleaning out a fridge right before a long trip." He grinned, then grabbed his cordless phone with his free hand and started to dial with his thumb.

"Who are you calling?" I asked as I dipped a Ritz in the petrified peanut butter.

"Your mother. We can't just leave without saying a word. I —"

Before he could finish, I swiped the phone and canceled the call.

"What the hell?" Grandpa Kalb said. "You got peanut butter all over my phone."

"And you almost blew the whole thing," I said. "You can't call my mom!"

"I have to. We have to tell her something."

"No, we don't. We don't have to tell her anything. There's a decent chance she'll forget that she even dropped me off here, just like she did with you."

"Don't say that. That's not true. Now hand over the phone,"

he said, reaching for it. "Trust me, it's fine. I'll just say that I want to watch you for the rest of your suspension."

"And why would you ever volunteer to do that?"

Grandpa Kalb slowly pulled his hand back. He obviously knew there were holes in his story but didn't want to give up on calling my mom just yet. He tapped his chin with his fingers while he tried to come up with an explanation. After a second, he slapped the counter and exclaimed, "Got it! I'll tell her that I want to because I want to help out, and because I think it could be a great bonding opportunity for the two of us."

"That's a fantastic story," I said with as much sarcasm as I could muster. "I could really see it being a great made-for-TV movie on the Hallmark channel. But I don't believe you for one second, and there's no way she would either. Clearly, you've never really tried to lie to her."

"Not really. Except for that time about a half-hour ago, when I told her I was doing great."

"Yeah, and that worked out really well, didn't it? She totally caught you in your lie. Trust *me*, if you call her, she'll break you in less than a minute and we won't even make it out the door. The best way to handle her—actually, the only way to handle her —is to never say a word."

"I don't know," he said, still wrestling with the decision.

"Look at it like this," I said, "no matter what we do, whether we call her or not, we're lying to her and she's gonna find out. So, why not go with the option that's more likely to work?"

After a few more seconds of hemming and hawing, he finally conceded. "Dammit! You're right. Fine."

"It's the smart move," I said and put the phone back on the counter.

"I know," he said, still bothered by it all. He took out his lingering frustrations on his roll of ham, which he finished in two angry bites. "All right, let's get the car."

"Let's do this," I said and followed Grandpa Kalb out of the apartment.

"There's gonna be people in Walter's room, so we're gonna need a plan," Grandpa Kalb said in a hushed voice as we headed down the hallway.

"Isn't the plan to just get the keys?" I asked in a muffled tone of my own. That was what we had decided on the way back to Grandpa Kalb's apartment. He would grab his things, and then we'd go to Walter's hospital room—which was on the opposite side of the complex from my grandpa's apartment tower and next to the assisted living quarters—swipe Walter's keys, and then hit the road.

"That's the objective, not the plan," Grandpa Kalb clarified. "The plan is how we achieve our objective. In any gray area situation like this, you always need a plan. It also never hurts to have a backup plan, but I think we'll be fine without one here."

"How many times have you been in 'gray area' situations like this?"

"It might surprise you, but I wasn't always the straight-arrow you see today."

"It actually does," I said, and wasn't being sarcastic. I had always kind of imagined that Grandpa Kalb came out of the womb as a grizzled hard-ass who only did things exactly by the book. You know, bald and bossy and telling the other toddlers that naptime ended two minutes earlier. That was the vision I had.

"Well, when I was your age," he said, "actually a few years younger than you, my brother and I used to hop the train all the way from Scranton and sneak into Yankee Stadium. Back then, they didn't have the same technology or even turnstiles. Most of the time, you could just climb over the outfield fence when no one was looking. Every once in a while, though, there was someone on guard and it took a few fake tears and a well-crafted story to the ticket taker, usually about getting separated from our parents, to get inside the stadium."

"Wow, and you asked if I was a sociopath."

"Not my finest moments, but I was young, poor, and really loved baseball, so the ends justified the means. It's also proof that a good plan can get you in or out, or any direction you want to go, of anything. So ... when you go inside that room and someone asks who you are, what are you gonna say?"

"I'M HIS GRANDSON," I said to the nice old lady waiting at the doorway to Walter's tiny room in the hospital wing of Punta Gorda Gardens. I averted my eyes, which had begun to tear up. I wasn't stirring up fake emotions; they were real. When I'd first peeked inside the room and saw Walter lying in the hospital bed, his eyes shut and his rigid body hooked up to a ventilator and some kind of IV drip, it reminded me of the last time I'd visited my grandma.

"I'm so sorry," the nice old lady said and rubbed my arm. "You poor thing. Can I give you a hug?" Before I could say yes or no, she blurted out, "I'm giving you a hug," and then leaned in and threw her arms around me.

While I was getting smothered by the elderly woman—and her generously applied perfume—I overheard Grandpa Kalb chatting with the only other male in the hospital room. They spoke in what they'd intended to be hushed voices; however, given their hearing issues, they could only hush so much. Even from ten feet away, their conversation was as clear as a song playing through headphones.

"So, where's the kid's mother?" the other man asked.

"Filling out paperwork," Grandpa Kalb said.

"I didn't even know Walter had a grandson. At least, he never mentioned having one."

"Yeah, well, besides the Yankees, there was really only one thing Walter talked about."

"Touché," the other man said with a chuckle.

With all the grieving older women in the room, I had a pretty good guess what that "one thing" was. Walter had been quite the ladies' man, even in his older years.

"Plus," Grandpa Kalb said, "you know how it is. Everyone here is always bragging about their grandkids. He probably didn't want to get involved in all of that malarkey."

"I seriously doubt that would be a problem. Get a look at the kid. I don't see anyone bragging about him."

"Hey! You never know. He could be a good student."

"Trust me, I wasn't a good student. There's no way that kid is."

Grandpa Kalb snorted derisively. "Well, I'm sure your grandkids aren't anything special either."

"Jeez," the other man said and raised his hands. "Why are you getting so defensive?"

"Because his grandpa is barely hanging on and you want to rip the kid to shreds, that's why."

"Sorry," the other man said. "I didn't mean anything by it." He started to leave the room, passing by me and the older woman, who was finally freeing me from her consoling clutches. He patted me on the shoulder. "Hey, sorry about your grandpa."

"Thanks," I said and let out a faint smile, pleasantly surprised that Grandpa Kalb had just defended me. The other man continued out the door. Still grinning a little, I nodded to my grandpa. He shot me an agitated glance that screamed: "What the hell are you doing? You're gonna blow your cover." I immediately wiped the enjoyment from my face, turned my gaze down to my feet, and stepped into the room.

"All right," Grandpa Kalb announced to the half-dozen or so mourners in the room, "we should probably let the kid have a minute alone with his grandpa."

Our plan worked just as we'd expected. The others agreed to give me some time alone, and Grandpa Kalb ushered them out of the room to help speed up the process. He gave me a "get to work" nod as he closed the door, and that's exactly what I did.

I started with the most obvious place: the two cardboard boxes that were labeled "Walter's Things." I found a lot of things —like clothes, a few grooming and hygiene supplies, and a slew of condoms and various "sexual enhancement" products—but not the thing that I was actually looking for.

I turned my attention to the nightstand next to Walter's hospital bed. There was nothing on the top or in the bottom compartment, and the small drawer it had was empty too. I searched the cabinets that lined the room, but all I found were random medical supplies.

As I scanned the room with my eyes, hoping to find my next place to search, I could hear more people outside, new arrivers who were already getting antsy.

"Well, how long do you think he needs?" one crotchety sounding man asked.

"I don't know," Grandpa Kalb said. "Give him some time. It's only been a few minutes."

"Well, I have water aerobics coming up shortly, and I can't be late."

I knew there was only so long that Grandpa Kalb could hold them off, and that, as old people like to say, I didn't have all day. I also didn't have any idea where to look next, as my short list of options was seemingly exhausted.

8

I heard the doorknob to the hospital room creak, twisting open just as I finished reorganizing some of Walter's things. The restless crowd waiting outside the room became markedly less anxious when they discovered me waiting inside with a sullen look on my face. I slipped past them and all of their condolences as I exited into the hall, where I was surprised to find that my grandpa was nowhere to be seen.

I spotted my hugging partner. "Where's my grandpa—" I stopped short, barely catching myself. "Grandpa's friend? Do you know where my grandpa's friend went?"

She pointed down the empty hall and said that he'd "hurried off" about a fifteen seconds earlier.

I briskly headed in the direction she'd gestured. As I rounded the corner of the first intersecting hallway, I located Grandpa Kalb. He was casually waiting by his suitcase, which was right where he'd stashed it, halfway down the hall and out of sight, before we stopped by Walter's room.

"What took you so long?" he said.

"Seriously?" I said. "You were supposed to stand guard."

"I was, for a while, but then I saw a couple orderlies cruising down the hall, all suspicious-like. I didn't want them to steal my suitcase."

"You really don't trust anyone, do you?"

"I trust a handful of people, or maybe half a handful. I don't know. I don't keep track and it depends on whose hands we're talking about. But, I can tell you one thing, I definitely don't trust any of the orderlies they got working at this joint. I know for a fact that they're stealing our meds and then giving us Canadian generics."

"Do you have proof?"

"If I had proof, they'd be doing hard time upstate, or wherever the big prison is here. What I got is years of experience, watching people and knowing what's up. That's what I got."

I just shook my head.

"You can shake your head till your brain turns to butter, but I'm right," Grandpa Kalb said. "Anyway, how'd it go?"

"Besides you leaving your post?"

"Yeah, besides that."

"Well, I got good news and bad news."

"Good news first. Always the good news."

"I got the keys," I said. I'd barely pulled it off too, no thanks to my grandpa. Just before I was joined by the gaggle of geezers, I'd noticed Walter's slacks hanging on the corner of his bed. Thankfully, I picked the right pocket, which happened to be the left one, to search first because I wouldn't have had time to check the other pocket.

Grandpa Kalb stared at me, confused. "I don't get it," he said. "If you got the keys and didn't get caught, what the hell's the bad news?"

I pulled the keys from my pocket. They were attached to a

white leather keychain that was stitched with red plastic around the edges and had 'NY' in blue, overlapping letters in the center. "We're driving a Buick," I groaned as I gave them a jingle.

"Are you kidding me?" Grandpa Kalb said with the same flabbergasted face I'd seen twice before when I ragged on baseball and his buddy Sinatra. "That's anything but bad news. I'll have you know that Buick makes, arguably, the finest American automobile out there. Sure, some people prefer Lincolns or Cadillacs, but I'd put my money on Buick. Just wait." He nodded and grinned. "You'll see, and you'll change your tune."

I'M NOT sure if it was necessary, but we snuck out one of the side doors so that no one witnessed our exit, and then scampered across the parking lot to the car. I climbed into the driver's side and started adjusting the seat, steering wheel, and mirrors. I stopped, my hand still on the rear-view mirror. I could feel my grandpa watching me from the shotgun seat. I turned to him sporting the same smirk as before.

"Well, what do you think now?" he asked. "Craftsmanship at its finest, right?"

I finished adjusting the rear-view mirror and then tested the seat, gently bouncing up and down. As much as I didn't want to agree with the old man, he was right. It wasn't just the seats either, everything about the car was well put together. Of course, I wasn't about to let him know that. "I guess it's pretty comfortable," I said, playing it down.

"You 'guess' it's pretty comfortable?" he snorted derisively. "Driving a Buick is like driving your living room couch. If your living room couch also had a dependable engine, was easy to give an oil change, and reasonably priced."

"Wow," I said. "You really do like Buicks."

"You're damn right I do."

"You should sell these. You'd be great at it."

"Yeah, right," he said. "Maybe in another life."

"I'm pretty sure you wouldn't have to wait for another life. Haven't you heard, it's never too late to change what you're doing and do what you want."

"That's really nice. Did you learn that in school?"

"Yeah."

"Well, congrats, because they've succeeded at shielding you from reality. That's not how the real world works at all. In the real world, when you start getting older, doors close. That's why you won't be seeing me shagging fly balls in the big leagues either."

"Sure, some doors might close, but not all of them, especially the selling Buicks door. I'd be willing to bet that one is always open. Or there's not even a door on there. It's just a big, wide-open entryway."

"Yeah, maybe," he said in passive agreement.

"I'm not even kidding," I said, "you'd be great at selling these."

"Thanks," Grandpa Kalb said with the first true smile I'd seen on his face in a while.

"If I had more savings and a license, of course, I'd probably buy one." I put the key in the ignition and was about to turn it when Grandpa Kalb grabbed my hand.

"Slow down, Cowboy," he said. "Speaking of that license. Since you only have your permit, before we even move one inch, you gotta pass my driver's test. First things first, where do your hands go?"

"On the wheel," I said with a smirk.

Grandpa Kalb wasn't amused. "Okay," he said while pretending to take notes on his palm, "that's five points off for the wrong answer and two more deducted for not taking this—"

"Ten and two," I said, cutting him off. "That's where your hands go."

"Much better. Keep them there at all times. Are you familiar with SMOG?"

I was tempted to make a quick joke about air pollution and carbon footprints. It was right on the tip of my tongue, but I thought better of it at the last second. "Yeah," I said. "It's the acronym for changing lanes. Signal. Mirrors. Over the shoulder. Go."

"Since you know what it means, let's see it in action."

I sighed and then demonstrated proper lane changing technique while Grandpa Kalb kept making fake notes in his fake palm notepad. I can only imagine what someone might have thought if they had passed by and spotted us in the car.

"Well?" I asked as he finished writing on his hand.

"It needs a little work," Grandpa Kalb said. "Specifically, on your over the shoulder look. You need to be quicker. We could have gotten in an accident with that lane change."

"We're parked."

"For now. When we're on the road, it's a totally different ball game."

It took a lot of effort to not roll my eyes or shake my head. Instead, I just said, "I'll keep that in mind and be quicker."

"Good. Because I'll be watching you."

"Great. Anything else?"

"Just one more thing," Grandpa Kalb said. "Last, but definitely not least, we need to talk about the speed limit. The speed limit is a limit, not a starting point or a suggestion. I want you to keep it five miles per hour under the designated limit at all times."

Growing up in South Florida, I was intimately familiar with the speed-conscious driving habits of old people, who made my mom look like Dale Earnhardt Jr. While they might have been "The Greatest Generation," they definitely didn't get that nickname from their work behind the wheel.

"Are you serious?" I said, hoping that he wasn't and that it was just a bad joke to kick off the trip.

"As serious as Good Friday mass," he said sternly. "We have three and a half days to get to New York. We don't need to be reckless. Plus, it's a much safer and smoother ride that way. When you get to be my age, you can get motion sickness from standing up too fast. Or even from just thinking about standing up too fast."

I shook my head in disbelief.

"All right," Grandpa Kalb said. "Well, whenever you're done shaking your head, we can ship out. Just keep the ship five miles under the limit."

I glanced at my right boot, which was resting on the gas pedal. My mind flashed back to the smile on Grace's face after she discovered the boots in the shoe bin at the Salvation Army. After a second, her smile disappeared, turned to a scowl, and she said, "It's over." Seeing the words come from her mouth, albeit imagined, hurt almost as bad as the text. I quickly banished the image from my head and returned my focus to the dash. I took a deep breath and then sighed. It was time to go, time to get away. Goodbye, Grace. Goodbye, Mom and Dad. Goodbye, Florida.

"I'm done," I said and threw the car into gear.

9

After less than five minutes on the freeway, there was already a long line of cars that had formed behind us. The cacophony of car horns that followed created the world's worst marching band, of which I was the drum major. I glanced in the rear-view to get a glimpse of the angry brass section that was steadily gaining members.

"Don't worry about them," Grandpa Kalb said. "Worry about yourself and those hands of yours. If that's what you call ten and two, something's wrong with your clock."

I looked at my hands, which had slipped to more of an eight and four. I moved them back to my grandpa's preferred position and did my best to focus on the road ahead. "We're—" I started before getting cut off by a rapid succession of honks from the driver just behind us. Once it passed, I continued, "We're really gonna do this all the way to New York?"

"It'll stop eventually," Grandpa Kalb said confidently.

"Yeah. When someone gets really bad road rage and runs us off the freeway."

"The only reason people get road rage—"

"Is driving like this?"

"No," Grandpa Kalb said with a glare. "It's because common courtesy is suddenly uncommon. No one gives 'the wave' anymore. A simple"—he raised his hand and gave a little flick-of-the-wrist wave—"would solve everything."

"I have a feeling that wouldn't make any difference."

"On the contrary. It would make all the difference in the world."

I glanced in the side-view mirror, where a Mercedes was coming up on our left. The driver was punching his horn like there was a chance that it might turn into my face. "How's this? I'll put your little theory to the test right now."

"Go right ahead. Just don't be too surprised when you find out I'm right."

"I don't see that being a problem." I turned to the driver of the Mercedes as he pulled up beside us. While he stared daggers at me, I calmly raised my hand and gave a friendly wave, just like my grandpa had demonstrated.

The gesture only infuriated the driver even more. "Screw you!" he screamed so loud that we were still able to hear it over all the horns, engines, and air whipping by. He flicked us off with both hands, and then gunned his car, continuing past us before cutting back into our lane with only inches between our bumpers.

"Jesus!" I said and tapped the brakes to make sure we didn't get clipped.

"Same to you, asshole," Grandpa Kalb shouted. He shook his head. "Some people."

"Really," I pretended to agree and then rolled my eyes. "So, about your little theory, I think you might be onto something."

"Please," he said, refusing to accept that his hypothesis had just been disproved. "That was just one car. It's too small of a sample size. Plus, you have to smile to make it work. You didn't smile."

"How do you know?"

"Because I could see your reflection in the window. You gotta smile, and it's gotta be genuine. That's what really sells the wave."

Just as soon as he finished his sentence, the honking came to a complete and sudden stop. A few seconds passed without a peep.

"Or maybe the smile is optional," Grandpa Kalb chuckled smugly. "See? What did I tell you? All it took was one wave, and then everyone realized we're good people. The honking is behind us, and we got nothing but peaceful driving all the way to New York."

Just then, I caught a flicker of light in the rear-view mirror: the bright red reflection caused by the sun bouncing off a highway patrolman's flashers. "The honking isn't the only thing behind us."

Grandpa Kalb twisted around in his seat to trace my gaze. "Son of a bitch," he whispered to himself as he witnessed what I'd been watching: All the other cars were moving out of the way, allowing the cruiser to speed up just behind us.

Grandpa Kalb whipped back around and dropped down in his seat. "Dammit!" he said as he pounded the passenger-side door with his fist. "I knew we should've taken surface streets!"

I could feel my heart beating in my hands as my fingers gripped the steering wheel even tighter. I kept one eye on the road and the other on the rear-view mirror. The officer in the passenger seat appeared to be entering our info into their system or something as they tailed us a few car lengths back.

"Both eyes on the road!" Grandpa Kalb said. He took a couple of deep breaths and then continued, "It's okay. Everything's okay. We're gonna be fine. Just stay calm, keep your hands and eyes where they are, and slow down."

"Slow down?" I exploded. "What? Why?"

"You always slow down whenever you see a police car! Everyone knows that!"

"Yeah, but that's only if you're going fast! We're already going slow to begin with!"

"It doesn't matter! Whatever speed you're going, fast or slow or somewhere in between, you still slow down. So, slow the hell down!"

"Fine!" I said through gritted teeth. I gently tapped the breaks, dropping the speedometer another five miles below the posted limit, for a grand total of ten.

A few seconds passed, and then Grandpa Kalb carefully contorted his body in the seat, attempting to get the proper angle on his side-view mirror that would allow him to spy on the cops. By the time he found it, his body bent halfway into the center console. "All right," he whispered. "We're looking good. Another couple seconds and we should be in the—"

Cut off by the whooping of the police siren, Grandpa Kalb shot up in his seat.

"Great!" I groaned as the cruiser's lights continued to flash red and white. "You're two for two now. You got any advice on how I should pull over?"

"Slowly."

"Of course. I should've guessed that." I shook my head and started to slow down.

As I veered toward the shoulder of the highway, the officer's voice blasted over their bullhorn speaker. "Sir," the officer announced in an almost robotic monotone, "you do not need to pull over. Just do a better job keeping with the flow of traffic."

I sighed. I couldn't believe we'd been that close to getting busted, and then somehow avoided it. I pulled back onto the road and gradually picked up speed. My hands were just starting to relax on the wheel, letting the blood return to my white knuckles, when Grandpa Kalb said, "We aren't out of the woods just yet."

I peered in the side-view mirror, monitoring the police cruiser as it crept up next to us. They pulled even. Out of the corner of my eye, I noted the officers in the car, an older man with a mustache who was behind the wheel and a younger female officer sitting beside him, glaring in our direction. The woman lowered her aviators down the bridge of her nose and narrowed her eyes, clearly looking for a reason to change their mind and pull us over.

"Give them a wave and smile," Grandpa Kalb mumbled through closed lips like a poorly trained ventriloquist.

I turned toward the cruiser, forced a smile so wide that the corners of my mouth could have kissed my earlobes, and waved. I watched the faint reflection of Grandpa Kalb in the window as he did the same.

"Now," Grandpa Kalb said, still keeping his mouth closed, "eyes back on the road."

I turned my head back to the road, leaving one eye on the officers. The driver turned back to the road too while his partner kept her focus on me and slowly pushed her shades back up to the top of her nose. The driver gunned the cruiser, and they took off down the highway, going damn near a hundred miles an hour.

"See!" Grandpa Kalb exclaimed. "You see what just

happened right there. All it took was a little wave, and it did the job."

I couldn't believe it. I wanted to scream. I felt like a steam engine, building pressure, preparing to whistle. His stupid rule about the speed limit had nearly gotten us pulled over before we even made it past the city limits. While his almost-as-stupid wave move had nothing to do with saving us, here he was trying to gloat like he knew everything. I somehow managed to restrain myself. "It sure did," I said with an equal mix of frustration and sarcasm, neither of which were detected by Grandpa Kalb.

"Yep. It worked like a charm," he said and grinned.

I shook my head and snorted derisively.

"What?" he asked. "You can't argue with the facts."

No longer able to contain myself, I unloaded everything that I'd been holding in. "The fact is, your wave is stupid and doesn't work! You almost got us busted, and you can't even admit that you're wrong! Are you senile? Have you ever considered that everything you think you know about the world, isn't even remotely close to being true anymore?"

The smile melted off his face like an ice cream cone in August. "Watch your damn mouth," Grandpa Kalb said. He turned, stared out of the passenger-side window, and then softly added, "And, yes, I have considered that. More often than you could even imagine."

He looked like a sad puppy. I would've felt sorry for him, but I forced myself not to—I'd had enough of his shit. He needed to be taken down a peg or two. If not, I knew I probably wouldn't even make it to Orlando without losing my mind. And even if I did, I still needed to assert myself; otherwise, he'd just keep ordering me around the whole trip.

Emboldened by Grandpa Kalb's show of weakness, as well as

the policeman's orders, I readjusted in my seat and let my hands slide to nine and three. "From now on," I said, "so we don't have any more run-ins with the cops, I'm going with the flow of traffic."

"Fine," he said. "Just no more than five miles over the limit."

"Five miles below. Five miles over. What's with you and the number five?"

"It's a great number. Joe DiMaggio wore number five."

"I have no idea who that is."

"He was only one of the best players to ever wear pinstripes," Grandpa Kalb said, turning around and getting some of his confidence back. "I'm might not know everything about the world today, but I know that. He still has the record for the longest hitting streak too. Probably will never be broken."

"Good for him," I said. "But I'm going with the flow of traffic, regardless of if it's within Joe DiMaggio's jersey number of the speed limit or not." I punched the gas, and the Buick took off, even more than I'd expected.

Grandpa Kalb's head jerked back into the seat cushion, and his hand gripped the door handle. I could feel him getting more and more uncomfortable as the gauge glided across the speed markers. I smiled inwardly, taking enjoyment in his discomfort.

10

Neither of us said much the rest of the way through Florida. Grandpa Kalb was clearly stinging from the reality check I'd given him, and I wasn't exactly looking to wind up the old chatterbox and get him talking again. I'd quickly determined that I enjoyed driving with him a lot more when he was quiet and I could just appreciate the rhythmic calm of the open road. And so, when he turned on some "golden oldies" radio station about fifteen minutes after our little squabble, I didn't even fight him over it. I just tuned it all out.

There were a couple of times where the lull of the road caused my mind to drift back to thoughts of Grace and the pain I was suppressing; however, for the most part, my lack of driving experience and my fear of messing up kept all of my attention firmly on the freeway.

About ten miles after crossing into Georgia, the fuel light came on and Grandpa Kalb instructed me to take the next exit. I pumped the gas while Grandpa Kalb went inside the station to pay. Through the window, I watched him shoot the breeze with the elderly gas station attendant, who looked to be about my grandpa's age, albeit much huskier and casually dressed, with his overalls and trucker hat. I would've bet all the money in my bank account that it was a boring back and forth about the recent spike in gas prices or housing market crash, two old-people favorites.

Several cars pulled into the lot while I was refueling. The vehicles varied, but the wary glances from the passengers were all the same. At first, I was confused as to why I was catching such strange looks, and then I caught my reflection in the car window, followed by the soft jingle of boot buckles. I realized that I stood out like a sore thumb with jet-black hair. I suppressed my desire to flick them off, not wanting to attract any added attention, and just smiled and waved. Grandpa Kalb's can't-fail move continued its streak of failing.

Every time, the locals snapped their heads to avert their eyes and then giggled to each other as they scurried toward the station. I remembered Absinthe's stories of hopping from town to town, thanks to his dad's military career, and the unwelcoming residents and bullies that he encountered with each move. I imagined he'd lived in plenty of places just like the one I was in—towns where he was never even given a chance.

After the pump clicked off, I removed the nozzle, twisted the cap back on the tank, and took a seat on the hood of the car. With nothing to distract me, I was powerless to my own thoughts. As I stared at the gas station, I was reminded of the first time I saw Grace. By "saw," I don't just mean see. At that point, we'd been in school together for almost six years, and I'd seen her thousands of times. But even though I'd seen her, I never truly saw her. It's kind of like how you can listen to a song and not really hear the words. Well, the night I saw her, I finally heard the words.

I was spending the night at Derek's house. *Hostel* had just come out on DVD, and Derek's cousin, who worked at the local Blockbuster video store, let us rent it without our parents' permission. A bad move in hindsight, since it did give me nightmares for three weeks.

After procuring the movie, we biked to the nearby gas station to load up on snacks. While Derek was grabbing sodas, I went to snag some chips, and that's where I saw Grace. She was with Midnight, who was still going by Gloria at the time. Both of them were in the beginning stages of their goth transformation: just some new clothes and a little makeup, but nothing too drastic. They were also in the middle of debating whether they should go with salt and vinegar chips or Cool Ranch Doritos.

"Break the tie," Grace said to me with a grin as she held up the bags.

I just froze. I was too focused on the words that I'd never heard from the song of Grace—*Amazing Grace*, and how sweet the sound—to hear the words she'd actually said.

Still smiling, Grace continued, "I mean, it's pretty obvious. Doritos, right?"

"You can't do that," Midnight insisted. "You just influenced his vote. That's cheating."

"No," I said, finally finding my voice, "I was going to say Doritos anyway. It's Cool Ranch, and it's not even close."

"Exactly," Grace said, smiling even wider.

I smiled back. Midnight just shook her head, and then they both headed for the checkout counter. I watched them from the back of the store, racking my brain and trying to determine why it had taken me so long to notice something that, at that point, seemed so obvious: Grace was the most beautiful person I'd ever seen.

After they left, I met back up with Derek. "Doritos?" he said as I handed him the chips. "I thought we agreed on barbeque Fritos?"

"I was craving Cool Ranch," I said with a shrug, leaving out the reason why.

Sitting on the hood of the car, I felt the same craving. My body demanded anything that could bring me closer to Grace. I was startled from my trance when Grandpa Kalb shouted, "What the hell are you doing?" He charged toward the car carrying a couple of plastic grocery bags filled with a random assortment of junk food. Unfortunately, as far as I could tell from the packaging peeking out of the bags, he'd left Cool Ranch Doritos off of his list. He continued his little tirade, "Don't sit on the hood like that. It's disrespectful to the workers who built it."

"Unless this car was built in the '70s," I said, "I'm pretty sure it was built by a machine."

"And someone obviously had to operate the machine."

"Yeah, a computer program."

"Well, at some point someone, a real-live, hardworking human being, designed something or wrote a program and put it together. So, don't sit on it." He arched his brows, lifting them halfway up his forehead to emphasize his point.

"Whatever," I said, not budging.

Grandpa Kalb glared at me for a second and then shook his head and rolled his eyes, accepting defeat. "Whatever is right. That seems to be your attitude toward everything. You're a goddamn pimple on the ass of progress," he said and then climbed into the car.

I waited a few seconds before sliding off the hood and then

took my time getting back into the Buick. I fired up the car and then spun the wheels as we pulled out of the station and onto the nearby highway ramp, leaving the town in a cloud of dust.

GRANDPA KALB and I had been back on the freeway for about five miles, when he turned the radio down and, completely out of left field, asked, "So ... how's school going?"

I shot him a scowl that in no uncertain terms said: Why the hell are you asking?

"Eyes on the road," he said. "I'm just making small talk."

I rolled my eyes and then turned my attention back to the asphalt artery. I knew my grandpa wasn't just "making small talk." The old man from Walter's hospital room had obviously planted a seed in his head. That seed had likely been fertilized by comments my grandpa overheard in the gas station and had sprouted into questions. And now, he wanted answers. "So how is it?" he asked again.

"It sucks," I said, deliberately keeping my response short.

"Sure. But you don't have any plans of like shooting up the place or anything, right?"

"Are you shitting me?" I said.

"Watch your mouth and don't act so surprised," he said. "You look exactly like one of them school shooters. Those Columbine kids."

"Those kids weren't goth," I said. I'd learned about the media-created myth the first day I hung out with Grace and her friends. It was one of the most overused stereotypes, which anyone who was goth was quick to debunk. "And I don't plan on doing anything like that." I thought about my real plan and how my grandpa might react when we got to New York and I disappeared. He was definitely in for a surprise.

"Whatever they were, they were assholes. I was just making sure. That's all."

I didn't respond. I was hoping we could just go back to not talking. I let a second of silence turn into two and then three, hoping that many more would follow and that we'd start a new silent streak that we could ride all the way to New York. We didn't. The streak stopped at four, when my grandpa asked, "So, are you getting good grades?"

"Yeah," I sighed. "Just because school sucks doesn't mean it isn't easy."

"Your mother used to say the same thing about school. Not that it sucked, but that it was easy. She still studied her tail off anyway."

"That doesn't surprise me."

"So, what's with the getup then?" Grandpa Kalb said. "I mean, I always say, 'Just be yourself, and if someone doesn't like you, tell them to go to Hell.' But you actually look like you might prefer that option. You know, going to Hell and all."

"It can't be any worse than this life. The world is a dark place, and just because all the conformists refuse to acknowledge that doesn't make it any less true." That's what I said, but they weren't really my words. They were Midnight's. She'd said it a few times. Although, I think she might have been quoting a book, so there's a chance they weren't her words either.

"So, you are into the Devil and all that kind of stuff then?"

"Yeah, I worship the Devil all the time," I said firmly, trying to get a reaction out of him. But it didn't, at least not as much as I had hoped or expected. I shook my head. I couldn't fake that. I wasn't into the Devil at all, and on the off chance that God—who I only kind of believed in—was listening, I didn't want him or her to get the wrong idea. "I'm just kidding. That's totally different."

"I see," he said in a voice that made it sound like he knew more than he really did. "So, basically, you're just trying to piss off your parents or something like that, right?"

"No."

"You sure about that?"

"Yeah." Of course, I was mad at my parents, and maybe that had been my initial intention, but it wasn't all about them. It had more to do with Grace than anything else, but I wasn't about to tell my grandpa that. I didn't want to tell him anything, but he just kept going.

"Not even a little?" Grandpa Kalb said, pushing harder. "I mean, you gotta be trying a little bit to piss off your parents."

"I couldn't piss off my parents if I wanted to," I said. "They don't give a damn about anything except for their careers, especially my mom."

"That's not true. That's not true at all."

"The first thing she said to me after I got busted was how it'd hurt her big election."

"She's right. And it is important."

"Exactly. It's more important than you or me."

"I don't know about that."

"It's true! Do you know the real reason she hasn't come to see you?"

"Well ... there are a lot of factors," Grandpa Kalb said, no longer so prodding or cocky. "It's complicated ... It's—"

"Because you're not in her voting district," I said plainly.

"If you were, she'd probably stop by every other week, maybe more. She'd be best buds with your neighbors and doing karaoke duets with Art. With my mom, there's her career and then there's everything else. She's just a selfish bitch."

While I might have had my grandpa on board with the first part of my rant, I definitely lost him with the last part. "Hey!" he barked, furiously shaking his finger at me. "Don't you call your mother a bitch."

I laughed off his little directive. "I'll call her whatever I want. Besides, calling her a bitch or not calling her a bitch doesn't change the fact that she is a total bitch."

"Call her a bitch again, and I swear I'll knock the taste, and every tooth, out of your goddamn mouth." Grandpa Kalb's clenched his jaw and cocked his fist.

I knew he wasn't kidding. But I wasn't about to back down. "You touch me," I said, "and I'll crash this damn Buick into the ditch. Then, assuming you can even walk after that, you can walk your ass all the way to New York."

Grandpa Kalb snorted derisively. "You don't have enough hair on those little beans of yours to do that."

"Only one way to find out," I said.

Grandpa Kalb glared at me. I glared right back. It was another chance for me to show him that I wasn't messing around, and I wasn't about to let it go to waste. I was going to win even if it meant crashing into the ditch.

After a couple of seconds, with neither of us backing down, Grandpa Kalb tried to force his way to a win. "I told you to keep your eyes on the road," he said.

Without saying a word, I kept them locked on him.

After a few more seconds, Grandpa Kalb grunted, shook his

head, and then turned back toward the highway. "Just don't call your mother a bitch."

I casually turned my gaze back to the road. With two straight wins in our battle of wills under my belt, I was feeling pretty damn good. I slouched to a more comfortable position in the seat and let my hands slide slightly below their ten and two positions, going for more of a nine and three.

11

Not only did my victory give me a nice boost of confidence, but it also bought me another hour of uninterrupted driving. We were about fifteen miles shy of Savannah when Grandpa Kalb finally broke his silence and said that it was getting too dark and it was time to call it a day. I pulled off at the next exit, and we hit up the nearby McDonald's to grab dinner.

I weighed my options while we waited in line. I'd just settled on the Big Mac meal when Grandpa Kalb leaned over and said, "Just so you know, your budget is three bucks."

"Are you kidding me?" I pointed to the menu. "I can't even get combo meal with that."

"Well, you would've gotten five bucks, but I had to deduct two dollars for attitude issues, poor language, and general insubordination. You want a great lesson for life? Don't bite the hand that feeds you or the hand that pays for the food that feeds you. Look on the bright side, you can still get a Happy Meal. Maybe that will help improve your mood."

Grandpa Kalb chuckled at his own joke. I didn't. I didn't find it as funny as Grandpa Kalb or the teenaged cashier who took my Happy Meal order and then smirked as he described the toy that came with it.

When Grandpa Kalb pulled out his wallet to pay for the meal, I noticed a picture of my grandma in the plastic picture holder. I only caught a sliver of the picture behind it, but I recognized the electric blue background: It was an old family picture of my parents and me. I also spotted the baseball tickets and a stack of twenties stuffed inside the center of the wallet. Grandpa Kalb caught me staring at the money and proclaimed that another good life lesson was that cash was king and that credit cards just led to debt and identity theft.

We inhaled our food and then drove to the Comfort Inn across the street. Grandpa Kalb checked us in—luckily, there was still one room with two queens left—and then we went to our room. Exhausted from the long day of driving, I plopped down on my bed, ready to pass out. The bedspread was a little stiff, almost like they'd sprayed it with starch, but the mattress was surprisingly comfortable, living up to the chain's name.

"Shoes off the bed," Grandpa Kalb said and slapped my feet off the bed as he passed by. "I bet it'll take you an hour to unbuckle all those things." He chuckled to himself.

I remained reclined while I loosened my boots and then kicked them off at the heels, letting them fall to the floor with thuds.

Grandpa Kalb grabbed the remote control from the TV stand and took a seat in the faux-leather armchair that was by the window. He turned on the TV and started surfing through the channels. "All right! Here we go," he said as he found the Yankees game.

"Whoa! Wait a second," I said, sitting up in bed. "I don't want to watch baseball."

"Too bad."

"We're already driving to watch the Yankees. Do you really need to watch every game along the way?"

"Actually, I do. I live by one rule: If the Yankees are on, I'm watching it."

"I'm pretty sure you live by a lot more rules than that. I've seen it firsthand."

"Fair point. But that's one of the big ones. Another big one is: Whoever has the clicker, controls the TV." He grinned as he waved the remote and then used it to turn up the volume a couple of bars.

"This is stupid. They're already up seven to one," I said, pointing to the score as it popped up on the bottom of the screen just before they cut to a commercial break.

"That's good, but it doesn't mean a damn thing. The White Sox still have fifteen outs. It ain't over till it's over."

"No shit," I said. "That's the most obvious thing I've ever heard."

"How many times do I have to tell you to watch your mouth?" Grandpa Kalb said sternly. "And of course it's obvious, that's the beauty of it. It's a quote from Yogi Berra. It happens to be one of his most famous lines."

"I'm pretty sure he only cared about pic-a-nic baskets, so I don't think it applies to this."

Grandpa Kalb shut his eyes, shook his head, and then reopened his eyes. "Yogi Berra, not Yogi Bear. He was a catcher for the Yankees. Wore number eight, in case you were wondering."

"I wasn't."

"Either way, he was easily the best backstop ever, and my

favorite player of all-time. Both for his game and his great quotes."

"I have a great quote for you," I said. "'Free HBO.' It's a quote from the sign outside of this hotel. I suggest we take them up on it."

"Good one. But even if this game were legitimately over, we wouldn't be watching any HBO. I told your mother I wouldn't let you watch TV."

"Isn't that what I'm doing right now?"

"No. You're not actually watching it. You're just complaining about it. There's a big difference," Grandpa Kalb said. "Besides, baseball is always exempt from any punishment. Your mother knows that."

"Awesome," I groaned.

"If you want, I can teach you about the game."

"I'd rather go to sleep."

"Suit yourself," Grandpa Kalb with a smirk. He grabbed a package of mini powdered donuts from his gas station haul, threw his legs up on the ottoman to get more comfortable, and then began to devour his donuts.

I watched him for a few seconds, unsure if he was getting more enjoyment from the game or screwing with me. I shook my head, peeled back the covers, and then climbed inside. I threw one of the extra pillows on top of my head to cancel out the light and noise. It was much more effective at blocking the light than my grandpa's cheers.

"That a boy, Jeter!" he shouted at the TV after some play that must have been marginally important or impressive. "Way to flash the leather!"

I squeezed the pillow even tighter around my ears, but it hardly made a difference. I should've known better. I'd unsuccessfully tried the same move many times before during my parents' biggest blowout fights. Even from my bedroom on the second floor, with my door shut and a pillow covering my ears, I had always been able to hear them go at it.

One time, I got so frustrated that I just screamed, "Will you two stop it already!" I was surprised when it actually worked. Their fighting ceased, albeit for a grand total of five seconds. Then they got back into it, even more fired up than before, their argument shifting to who was more responsible for upsetting me.

That night, I realized that most of my parents' arguments weren't even over what they appeared to be about. While they might have seemed to be over who left a sock in the living room or who deleted some show from the DVR, they were really the culmination of a history of small and unresolved issues that were left to fester and then unloaded at once. I also realized that there were no winners in those kinds of arguments, only losers, and the losers were both of my parents and me.

My parents' worst fights replayed in my head like a painful greatest hits CD, until my exhausted body finally saved me from my mind, and I passed out.

THE NEXT MORNING, I woke up to the sound of Grandpa Kalb mumbling something to himself. I opened my eyes just enough to get a hazy glimpse of him sitting in the armchair, staring at his open wallet and the picture of my grandma.

"I miss you so much," he said and then closed his wallet and looked in my direction.

I quickly closed my eyes again. I had every intention of

staying in bed for another twenty minutes or more, maybe even falling back asleep. My plans were crushed almost immediately as I was hit with what felt like a spotlight.

"Rise and shine," Grandpa Kalb said, standing by the window and holding the curtain open just enough to let in the thick slab of light that cut across my face.

I raised my hand to block the beam, turned to the nightstand, and with blurry eyes, checked the time on the old alarm clock. It was barely after seven, which was earlier than I even woke up for school. "What the hell are you doing?" I groaned.

"Is it not obvious? I'm waking your keister up," Grandpa Kalb said. "The early bird already got the worm and is even going back for seconds."

"Good for the early bird," I said and pulled the covers over my head. I was expecting Grandpa Kalb to rip them off and start the day with some more arguing.

But he didn't.

After a few seconds under the covers, I peeked out and saw he had already passed by and was retrieving a large, plastic container from his suitcase. The tackle-box-looking container wasn't much smaller than the suitcase itself. He unlatched the lid and then grabbed a handful of pills, plucking them one at a time from their various compartments.

I sat up in bed. "You got enough pills there?" I said, trying to get a rise out of my grandpa.

"Just enough," Grandpa Kalb said, not taking the bait. "Only what the doctor gave." He tossed them into his mouth and washed them down with a couple of gulps of Mountain Dew. He then tore open a Twinkie package and took a bite, still chewing while he filled a syringe with some clear liquid from a tiny glass bottle.

"And you said I was an addict," I said, firing another shot. But that didn't get any reaction either. So, I tried one more time. "You ever think your health problems might be related to that diet of yours?"

Grandpa Kalb considered my words for a moment and then took another bite of his Twinkie. "Doubt it," he said in between chomps. He polished off the last of his Twinkie and then plunged the syringe needle into his abdomen and emptied the contents. "Besides," he said as he started to put his medical supplies away, "I actually haven't eaten like this in years. Your grandmother would've never let me have this stuff. She watched over my diet like a hawk. I'm just taking a little break. You know, trying to live a little and have some fun."

"Oh."

"Care for a breakfast Twinkie?" he asked with a friendly grin. It was almost too friendly. Not taking any of the bait I'd laid out to kick off our quarreling was one thing, but it was almost like he had totally forgotten everything that had happened between us the day before, like we hadn't butted heads.

I was equally confused by his demeanor as I was by the concept of his breakfast Twinkies. "Is that what those are?"

"Yeah."

"I didn't even know they made breakfast Twinkies."

"Oh, yeah, they've been making them for years. It's actually the same recipe as a regular Twinkie, you just eat them for breakfast." Like he'd done dozens of times before, Grandpa Kalb chuckled at his own joke.

I shook my head. I couldn't help but smile. Not at the joke, but how much he enjoyed it.

"I can't take credit for that one," Grandpa Kalb said. "It's an old co-worker's joke. He had a breakfast Twinkie every morning.

Passed away at fifty-seven, but I was surprised he even made it that long. So, you want one?"

"Sure," I said.

Grandpa Kalb tossed me the Twinkie. "Dewski to wash it down?" he said, holding up a 20-ounce Mountain Dew.

"Why not?" I said and then caught the tossed soda too.

"I was thinking about it," Grandpa Kalb said and then took a sip from his beverage. "And we're kind of like fugitives or missing persons. It's only a matter of time before they put out an APB on us."

"APB?"

"All-points bulletin. You know, to be on the lookout for us. Once that's out there, we'll have the cops, feds, you name it searching for us, assuming they aren't on our asses already. So, before we hit the road, we should probably take some evasive measures."

"Like what?"

"Well, we need to ditch our plates for starters. But we also need to do something to change our appearance. We need to go incognito."

"I don't know about that," I said. I knew he was probably right about needing disguises, but my clothes and boots all reminded me of Grace, particularly the good times that we'd had. As much as she'd hurt me, I wasn't ready to let go.

"Listen," Grandpa Kalb said, "you were right about not calling your mother, and now I'm right about this. Looking like we do, they'll round us up in no time. All they have to do is tell everyone to be on the lookout for an incredibly handsome older man and a dark-clothed teenager with a bad dye job, and they'll find us in an hour tops."

I glared at my grandpa.

"Come on," he said, grinning. "That was just a joke. You really need to lighten up. And don't worry about the disguises. It's all temporary."

"Fine," I said.

"Perfect," Grandpa Kalb said, wiggling his eyebrows as he patted me on the back. "I already got it all planned out."

12

A fter making me wash off my makeup and comb my hair, we checked out of the hotel and then went to the local consignment store. I sifted through the racks of clothes. Each hanger flick kicked up a faint cloud of dust and a similar, yet unique, musty odor to go along with it. Both sent my allergies into overdrive. Even if my allergies hadn't been acting up, it still would've still been a bust. Thrift shopping just wasn't the same without Grace, who would overflow with excitement when she found something she liked, making even the oldest outfit seem brand-new. Without her, the clothes couldn't hide their age or their many other flaws.

"I didn't find anything," I said, stifling a sneeze as I approached Grandpa Kalb, who was waiting at the end of the row.

"That's okay because I did," he said, holding up a blue and white plaid short-sleeved button-up and a pair of pleated khaki shorts. It looked like something some third-grader's mom would've picked out for school pictures ten years ago.

"No way," I said. "Not happening."

"Why not?"

"Those are terrible."

"It's just clothes," he said. "You can always take them off."

I shook my head, standing my ground.

Grandpa Kalb continued, "I'd get you something black, but it would pretty much negate the whole disguise thing. The whole purpose is for it to be different. And this is about as different as you can get from what you're wearing. No one is gonna recognize you in this. Am I right or am I right?"

As much as I didn't want to admit it, he was right. "Fine," I said and yanked the clothes from my grandpa.

"I also need your shoe size," Grandpa Kalb called after me as I headed toward the dressing room. "So I can get you a new pair of sneakers."

I WAITED in the car in my new outfit, while Grandpa Kalb paid for the clothes and chatted up the lady at the register. On my grandpa's insistence, I'd tucked the shirt into my shorts. He claimed it was a necessary part of the overall look, which most people would probably describe as the look of "a kid who gets his ass kicked a lot."

My disguise was topped off with a pair of well-worn, white —turned off-white—Reeboks; although, bottomed off might've been a better way to describe their addition, since they were on my feet and were also possibly the worst part of the whole outfit. While wearing my secondhand boots hadn't seemed like a big deal, there was definitely something unsettling about having my feet in someone else's old, sweaty sneakers. I could only imagine how many rec center basketball games had been lost in these shoes. If I had anything going for me, it was that my grandpa let me keep my own boxers. I don't think water can even get hot enough to wash away the weirdness that comes with wearing used underwear.

After a minute, Grandpa Kalb exited the store carrying a large paper bag, which he tossed in the backseat of the car. "I got your old clothes, and I also got you a couple of extra shirts too," he said as he climbed into the passenger seat.

"Great," I said, rolling my eyes. "I can only hope they're as nice as this one."

"I don't think you'll be disappointed."

"Are we going to get the plates now?"

"We need to make one more stop before the plates," he said.

I followed his eyes, which were aimed at the top of my head. "No way," I said. "Not happening. That's not a temporary change. It took months to grow my hair like this."

"Hey," he said. "I'm not asking you to lop it all off. I just think you need to clean it up a little. That's all."

I checked out my hair in the rear-view mirror. I had to admit that it was a little uneven. Grace was hardly a pro and had missed a few patches when she buzzed the sides. To be completely honest, it looked like it had been cut with a weed wacker. A touch up couldn't hurt. Besides, Grace had also mentioned something about getting the top trimmed to fix my split ends, whatever that meant. "All right," I said, "but only a trim."

"A trim works for me," Grandpa Kalb said. "I'll even let you do all the talking."

"If you don't, I walk," I said.

"We can pinky swear if you want to." He held out his hand.

I looked at his finger for a second, rolled my eyes, and then fired up the car.

We drove along the tiny downtown strip of stores until we came across a barbershop with one of those old-time candy-cane-looking barber's poles hanging out front.

"Remember, I'm doing the talking," I said as I closed the car door and then started toward the entrance.

"Relax," Grandpa Kalb said and pulled open the front door to the barbershop and held it for me. "My memory isn't that bad."

"We'll see," I said and entered the barbershop.

Inside were four older African-American men. One was getting a haircut, another was doing the cutting, and the other two were just hanging out in the old-fashioned, leather barber's chairs that lined both sides of the room. All of them were laughing uproariously. At least they were until they noticed Grandpa Kalb and me, and then their howling came to a sudden halt.

"Whoops, wrong place," Grandpa Kalb said. "Sorry to interrupt."

Before I could say anything, he grabbed me by the shoulder and yanked me back outside.

"What the hell are you doing?" I said, finally pulling myself free from my grandpa's grasp. "I was supposed to do all the talking."

"I know. But you don't want to get your haircut there," he said adamantly.

"Why because they're African-American?"

Grandpa Kalb swayed his head side to side. "Yeah ... that's part of it."

"Seriously?" I said, disappointed in my grandpa. "That's racist."

"I'm not racist!" he shot back. "I have lots of black friends."

"That's what racist people say."

"No, they don't. If you call a racist person racist, they just say, 'So what?' Because they don't care, because they're assholes in the first place."

I rolled my eyes, even though it was actually a decent point.

Grandpa Kalb continued his defense, "Remember the breakfast Twinkie story? Well, my friend who came up with that was black."

"No, he wasn't," I said, calling his bluff just for the hell of it.

"Fine. Maybe he wasn't. But I still have a lot of black friends. And a lot of my favorite Yankees are black. Heck, I cheered for Jackie Robinson, even though he wasn't a Yankee." He arched his eyebrows and made a face as if to say that this was some game-changing piece of evidence, like a rock-solid alibi, that somehow proved his innocence.

"So, then why don't you want me to get my hair cut here?"

"Because"—he took a deep breath, weighed his words carefully—"I know this isn't a politically correct thing to say, but everyone cuts hair differently and likes different haircuts. A black guy is always gonna prefer a barber who cuts more black people's hair, and a white guy is gonna prefer a barber who cuts more white people's hair. Just like a Puerto Rican might—well, actually a Puerto Rican could probably go to either. Same for an Italian guy. They both have their own—"

"This is ridiculous," I said, cutting him off. "That might have been the case in the '50s, but it's 2008. I think anyone can cut anyone's hair."

This wasn't about just hair anymore. It was about the fact

that his "good old days" weren't as good as he thought they were, and that today and the future were better and brighter. It was about equality, progress, and yes, to a lesser extent, hair.

"We're gonna go back in there," I said with enough authority to let him know I wasn't changing my mind, "and I'm gonna get my hair trimmed by one of those highly skilled barbers."

Grandpa Kalb sighed and goal-posted his arms. "Hey. Whatever you say. It's your head."

I opened the door and reentered the barbershop. It was the same thing all over again. The laughter was a little quieter, but it ceased just as abruptly.

"I need a haircut," I said.

The three barbers, and even the man getting a cut, shared surprised looks. Through a series of shrugs and hand gestures, the two off-duty barbers debated who was going to take the job. They went back and forth for a while until the one closest to the entrance finally stood up.

"We're gonna let RT handle this," he said. "Just hop in a chair, and I'll go grab RT."

The barber disappeared into the back room, and I took a seat in the chair next to the only other patron. A few seconds of awkward silence passed and then Grandpa Kalb said, "Nice weather we're having, right?"

Everyone agreed, shaking their heads and offering their own compliments on the weather.

A few more silent seconds later, the other barber returned with RT, who was by far the oldest of the quartet and sported a white horseshoe haircut and a bushy mustache to match.

RT strolled over to my chair. "You need a haircut," he said, "or you need them all cut?"

"That's a classic," Grandpa Kalb chuckled. "I wish I was a barber just for that joke."

"Yep," RT said. "Unlike us, it never gets old."

"That's the truth."

"The truth is the only thing I know."

I cleared my throat to break up their old-man bonding session. "I need them all cut," I said. "But just a trim. That's it. Nothing crazy."

RT rubbed his chin and nodded while he sized up the task before him. "Don't worry, young buck," he said and then winked. "I got this." He spun my chair around, and then called to one of the other barbers, "Get me the scissors."

The fact that they appeared to only possess one pair of scissors and that someone actually had to leave the room to go get them, should have been enough to get me out of the chair and running for cover. However, I obviously didn't want to offend RT or the other barbers. I also had a point that I needed to prove to my grandpa, and there was no way I was going to let him think that he'd been right. So, I just sat through it, my hands gripping the handles of the barber chair as RT went to work.

"Whoopsie," RT said before the scissor blades had even finished their first snip.

Unfortunately, it would only be the first of many more whoopsies.

A HALF-HOUR LATER, I stared at my new crew cut in the reflection of the Buick window while Grandpa Kalb switched out the Florida plates with the Georgia plates he'd pulled from one of the many abandoned cars in the junkyard where we'd parked. One too many "whoopsies" had left my hair unsalvageable. Eventually, RT had to come in with the clippers to "even it all out."

"That about does it," Grandpa Kalb said as he finished tightening the license plate.

"This is terrible," I said, shaking my head as I continued to study my reflection. I was equally angered by how I looked and the fact that my grandpa had been right.

Grandpa Kalb sidled up next to me, matching my gaze in the window, and grinned. "I don't know what you're talking about," he said. "I think you look as sharp as a tack."

"Are you kidding me? I look like Forrest Gump!" It wasn't even an exaggeration. The clothes, the haircut, everything was a dead ringer for Forrest Gump.

"Watch your mouth," Grandpa Kalb said and then considered my comparison for a second. "I don't know. Say life is like a barbershop haircut, you never know what you're gonna get."

I stared daggers at my grandpa.

"Yeah, I don't see it," Grandpa Kalb said, stifling laughter. "Forrest had a much more pleasant disposition. It didn't matter what life threw at him, he stayed even."

"Screw you."

"Hey! Relax. The important part is that now no one will ever recognize you."

"How could they? I don't even recognize myself." I honestly recognized myself less with my buzzed head than I had with freshly dyed black hair.

"That's just a testament to how great the disguise is," he said, nodding his head. He patted me on the back a couple times. "Now, whenever you're done admiring yourself, we can hit the road, Forrest—I mean, Jordan." He giggled to himself as he walked around the car and climbed in the passenger's side.

I stewed for a few more seconds. After joining him in the car, I slammed the door as hard as I could. I'd never slammed anything so hard.

"Hey," Grandpa Kalb said, "don't take your anger out on the Buick. Just get this baby back on the road and let's get going."

"Whatever," I said and then jammed the key into the ignition. I started to turn the key but stopped, mid-twist. Something crossing my mind. Something wasn't right. Something hadn't been addressed, and I didn't realize it until just then. "Wait a goddamn second," I said. "What about your disguise?"

"I've already got that covered," he said, posing as he stroked his chin. "I'm growing a beard."

"Are you kidding me?"

"No. I've only had a beard once in my whole life. No one is expecting that.

"Yeah, but it'll be a week before you even have any real stubble."

"Hmmm," Grandpa Kalb said, playing dumb and doing a poor job of it. "I guess you're right. Well, it's a good thing all old people are pretty much invisible to everyone."

I could feel my cheeks getting warm as my face turned bright red, like a thermometer in a cartoon before it explodes. My jaw was clenched so tightly that my teeth could've cut metal.

Grandpa Kalb just continued, keeping up his guise as if it was working, "Maybe I should use an alias to be safe though. You can call me Al, like the Paul Simon song."

"How about I call you Dick?" I said through gritted teeth.

"I prefer Al. It was my dad's name. Well, really it was Albert, but he always went by Al."

I was over our bogus back and forth. If he was going to keep playing dumb, I was going to be smart and get out of my ridiculous new clothes. While he continued rambling about his dad, I reached over the seat into the back of the car and rifled through the paper bag stuffed with clothes. But all I found was more shirts and shorts like the horrible ones I was wearing.

I plopped back into my seat and smacked the steering wheel. "What the hell did you do with my clothes?" I demanded.

"I had the store manager burn them," Grandpa Kalb said.

I glared at my grandpa.

"What?" he said innocently, still sticking with his stupid act. "To get rid of the evidence. You never keep the evidence." As much as he tried to keep a straight face, he couldn't help but let out a little smirk and show his cards.

I realized that it had been his plan the whole time, and I had walked right into it. He'd been working me from the moment we woke up. "I can't believe I fell for this!" I screamed and ripped my shirt untucked.

"Fell for what? I have no idea what you're talking about."

"Don't play dumb with me! These stupid clothes, this terrible haircut, and even you being nice to me, it was all part of your plan!"

"Whoa, whoa, whoa," he said, finally giving up his facade. "I don't deserve credit for the haircut. Sure, I planned the clothes and cleaning you up a little, but that buzz cut is all you. If you don't remember, I tried to talk you out of it, and you said I was racist."

"Whatever," I said. Even though he was right, it was still his fault. He was the one that put me in that position. I wasn't as mad about the clothes as I was the fact that he had tricked me and that I had been so blind. The one thing I did want though was the boots. They were my last connection to Grace. But, thanks to my grandpa, that connection was gone for good. I huffed and puffed while he continued to grin.

"Although, I actually think RT did a decent job."

"Don't talk to me."

"After he botched it, of course. That first attempt was pretty terrible."

"I said don't talk to me!" I wrenched the ignition, firing up the engine to drown out any potential response from my grandpa, and then yanked the car in gear.

13

We shot past Savannah and into South Carolina. Every fifteen minutes or so, Grandpa Kalb would make a random comment. Usually, it was just something about the scenery, how it looked like it might rain, or a complaint about some aggressive driver. Every time, I just quietly sipped my soda and did my best to block out my grandpa and the Oldies music blaring over the radio. There were a few times when my anger actually started to subside, and then a lane change and resulting glance in the rearview mirror reminded me of my makeover and refueled my fury and vow of silence.

After about an hour and a half, we passed a sign indicating that Florence was only seventy miles away. "Evelyn had a good friend named Florence," Grandpa Kalb said to himself and then turned to me. "Yep. Your grandmother and Flo were like two peas in a pod." He paused, waiting for me to say something. After I didn't, he just continued, "I don't know about you, but I'm starving. This junk food just ain't gonna cut it. I need something more substantial. So, if you wanna take this exit up ahead and grab some real food, I'm on board."

I didn't respond. I just kept my eyes on the road and took another sip from my soda.

"Okay," Grandpa Kalb said after a couple seconds of silence. "If you wanna keep this little silent game going, that's fine by me. But if you are hungry, you don't have to say anything, just take this exit right here."

I blew by the exit, watching Grandpa Kalb's head turn as the exit came and went.

"We can always go to the next one," he said. "Or even see what else is up ahead. My stomach is starting to ache a little, but I could maybe hold out for fifteen minutes or so. Plus, there might be some better options down the road."

For the next hour, Grandpa Kalb announced every exit and its advertised food options. He took particular interest in the many iterations of the KFC, Pizza Hut, and Taco Bell combinations that were offered. He also made a point to note every Waffle House that we passed. It was more than apparent that he had an affinity for the establishment. It was equally apparent, at least to me, that there was no way in hell we'd be stopping at one. It didn't matter that I also loved Waffle House and was actually craving waffles. I was more than willing to deprive myself for the mere fact that it would potentially deprive my grandpa even more.

I'd seen my parents resort to this extreme tactic many times leading up to their separation. It had been the next-to-last stage in the evolution of their arguing. Surprisingly, the last stage in the deterioration of their relationship was an abrupt break in the action. While I'd incorrectly assumed, or hoped, that it was a cooling-off period and they'd turned the corner, in reality, they were really just trying to figure out how to break the news to me, which they ended up doing over frigging Frappuccinos at Starbucks—another place that I had no intention of stopping at.

"Waffle House coming up," Grandpa Kalb said with a tinge of pain in his voice as we approached yet another exit sign advertising the restaurant. Just like the exits earlier, I gave the Buick a little extra gas as we flew right by the off-ramp. "And there she goes," he said. "You realize that there are people in this country who have to drive hundreds of miles just to get to one Waffle House, and you've just driven by eight?"

I kept my mouth shut, not even dignifying his question with a slight glance.

Grandpa Kalb shook his head. "It's crazy. That's all I'm—" He stopped short and doubled over, moaning. "Okay, that was sharp. This is getting to be too much. I don't think my old stomach can't take it much longer."

I know it's sick, but after everything he'd put me through, I took a bit of pleasure seeing him in pain. After he moaned for a good thirty seconds, I finally opened my mouth and broke my monk-like silence. "Maybe you should've thought about that before you threw away my clothes and tricked me into getting this damn haircut," I said.

"I know," he groaned, still hunched over. "I know. I know. I should've thought about it. If only"—he calmly sat up—"I did." He smirked. I spotted powdered donut residue in the corner of his mouth. He licked it away with his tongue.

"What the hell are you talking about?" The possibility that he'd been pulling one over on me again hadn't crossed my mind.

"I'm talking about the fact that I'm not really that hungry. I mean, I could eat, but I also don't mind eating just junk food. I could probably live off it all the way to New York. The break was more for you, to stretch your legs and get a bite. Of course, I knew you probably wouldn't agree if I suggested it. So, I figured I would anyway and then see how long you could hold out. I'm actually pretty impressed. With the way you've been polishing off those Dewskis—I think that's your third bottle—I'm surprised you haven't needed a bathroom break yet."

Just like how you never notice a sound, like say a buzzing refrigerator or loud ceiling fan, until someone points it out, and then once they do, you can't stop noticing it, I hadn't even thought about needing to go to the bathroom or how much soda I'd drank until Grandpa Kalb brought it up. As soon as it entered my consciousness, it was all I could think about, and the pain in my lower abdomen went from nonexistent to unbearable in a matter of seconds.

"I spoke too soon," Grandpa Kalb said with a grin, "You look like you need to go pretty bad right now. Too bad that the exit we just passed was the last one for thirty miles."

Thinking about waiting thirty miles sent even more pains through my bladder, but I wasn't ready to give up just yet. "You're gonna need to go too," I said. "You've been drinking just as much as me."

"True. But there's one key difference between us. I put a fresh adult diaper on this morning to prepare for the long drive. I've been going this whole time."

I tried to conceal my discomfort, flexing every muscle in my face to keep from wincing.

"Yep," Grandpa Kalb said as he threw his hands behind his head confidently, "I got a good feeling I'm gonna be winning this little pissing contest of ours. Pun intended. Just don't think about rivers or waterfalls or the sound that they make. Pssssshhhh."

His smile and the twinkle in his eyes grew as he continued making his waterfall sound effect, and so did the sharp cramps stabbing my bladder.

———————

THE ACHING DIDN'T COMPLETELY DISAPPEAR until after I had finished relieving myself in the Cracker Barrel bathroom, washed and rinsed my hands in the sink, and then was halfway through drying them. Only then did I finally get the physical relief I had desperately needed. However, from a mental standpoint, I was anything but relieved.

I exited the bathroom and, with a scowl on my face that frightened the other customers in my path, plodded to the booth in the back of the kitschy restaurant where Grandpa Kalb was waiting. I don't know who opened the first Cracker Barrel, but I imagine it was someone who couldn't make up their mind if they wanted to open a restaurant that sells comfort food or just have a really big garage sale, so they decided to do both.

"Wow, that was a long one," Grandpa Kalb said, as I slid into the seat across from him. "You really should've timed it. It might have been a Guinness World Record. I don't know if kids are into that kind of stuff anymore, but I actually know the guy who has the record for the longest time on a Pogo stick. At least he did back in 1973 when he set the record. It wasn't exactly like Roger Maris getting the home run record, but it was kinda neat."

I said nothing, and Grandpa Kalb went back to perusing the menu and talking to himself.

A minute later, we were joined by our bubbly waitress. She was petite, in her early twenties, and eager to get our orders.

Grandpa Kalb went first. "I'll have the Uncle Herschel's Favorite with hashbrown casserole and ... well, I can't decide if I should go with the pork chop or catfish."

"I like the catfish," the waitress said.

"Catfish it is."

The waitress scribbled the order on a notepad and then turned to me. "What about you?"

I smiled, in anticipation of how my grandpa was going to respond, and said, "I'll just have the waffles."

"What?" Grandpa Kalb exclaimed, throwing his hands in the air. It was just the reaction I'd hoped for. "Seriously? And you didn't want to stop at the Waffle House? Are you crazy?"

That waitress snickered at Grandpa Kalb's antics. "You're sure you want the waffles?" she asked me. "I mean, I'd never say anything bad about our waffles, but he's right. You're cute, but he's right."

"Of course, I'm right," Grandpa Kalb said.

"Yeah. I'll stick with the waffles." I said and handed the waitress my menu.

She said she'd put the order in and then headed off.

As soon as she was gone, Grandpa Kalb slapped my arm and wiggled his eyebrows. "You hear that?" he said. "She called you cute. I'm telling you, the ladies are really gonna like that new look of yours."

"Not all of them," I said and averted my eyes.

A few seconds passed and then Grandpa Kalb said, "Well, I'll be damned." While I wasn't looking at him, I could feel the grin growing on his face through the excitement in his words. "All this weird stuff was about a girl. That's why you're so pissed off about your hair and clothes."

"No," I said.

"Who do you think you're fooling?"

"I mean, it wasn't just for her. I liked the way I looked, for the most part."

"Yeah, sure you did, and I like having to wear adult diapers." Grandpa Kalb laughed so hard that he began to lose his breath. "Oh, my God. I don't know how I didn't see it sooner. It's so obvious."

Each wheeze fanned my growing fury. It was bad enough to be tricked by him. I didn't need the humiliation. He kept bringing it though, laughing with no sign of stopping. I knew that he probably wouldn't stop the rest of the way to New York. I couldn't imagine it going on for a few more days, let alone a few more minutes. It's not what I had signed up for, for all of his games and bullshit. Little did he know, he was poking at the last stable piece in a wobbling Jenga tower.

"It was a girl," he said as tears started to stream down his face.

With that, the tower crumbled. I was done with his games, with his rules, and, most of all, I was done with him. I was ready to bring an end to everything. At least everything for him. And, as the entrance bell rang and two police officers stepped to the hostess' podium, I decided that's what it was time to do. I grinned, knowing that he was going down and that his own trick would be his downfall. I had a disguise, and he didn't. I could give him up to the cops and slip away unnoticed. Sure, I'd have to ditch the car, but I could find another way to New York.

I grabbed the napkin from my lap, tossed it on the table, and started to get up.

Grandpa Kalb traced my gaze to the police officers. His face dropped. "Whoa," he said, his voice squeaking from the nerves. "What are you doing?"

"I'm ending your trip."

"Why? Aren't we having fun? Isn't this just some good-natured ribbing?"

"No," I said and climbed out of the booth.

14

I started toward the two officers but only made it one step before I was stopped in my tracks. It was as if I'd run into an imaginary wall. In reality, it was just Grandpa Kalb. He had snagged a fistful of my shirt and was holding on for dear life.

"Don't do it," he begged as he strained to pull me back. "Stop."

"Let go," I snarled and yanked my shirt free. "It's over." I took another step and was about to raise my hand to signal the police officers when I heard the one thing that I never expected to hear.

I wouldn't have been nearly surprised if Grandpa Kalb had told me to "sit my sorry ass down" or that he was gonna "whip my keister." But his words weren't even close to as hostile as I'd anticipated, and neither was his tone. Of course, I knew there was a chance that I'd misheard him, and so I still needed a confirmation that my ears hadn't deceived me.

I stopped and turned back to him. "Excuse me," I said. "What did you say?"

"I said I'm sorry," Grandpa Kalb sheepishly replied,

repeating exactly what I thought I'd heard. "I wasn't laughing at you. Please, just sit back down. Let's talk it out. At least give me one more chance." He looked down at his hands and fumbled with his fingers. This raw and emotional side of Grandpa Kalb, I'd only seen briefly after our first run-in with the police.

"I'm not sitting down," I said. "Not yet." I took a step toward the table, making sure I was still out of his reach, in case I changed my mind.

Grandpa Kalb slowly lifted his head and sighed. "I'm sorry for busting your chops," he said. "But more than that, I'm sorry for tricking you into getting your haircut. If I'd known it was for a girl, I never would've done anything. Trust me. I'd never get in the way of love." His remorse was genuine. It was clear that he was telling the truth.

"Thanks," I said, forgiving him just a tiny bit, enough that I stopped tracking the cops out of the corner of my eye. "Not that your apology changes anything."

"I know it doesn't. But it'll all grow back, and I'll give you some money for new clothes and shoes. You don't have to dress like Forrest Gump."

"Good," I said. "Because I'm done with these clothes. I'm also done fighting with you."

"No more fighting or tricks. I promise."

I hesitantly took a seat back in the booth.

"Thank you," Grandpa Kalb said and nodded gently. We both sat silent for a second and then Grandpa Kalb nodded more firmly and said, "Well ..."

"Well, what?" I said.

"Tell me about this girl. Or do you want me to guess? I'd go out on a limb and guess dark hair, dark clothes, dark attitude." He let out a faint smirk, letting me know it was just a joke.

I grinned and shook my head. "She doesn't have a 'dark' attitude. She's actually really sweet and super smart."

"Good. Sweet and smart are two top-notch qualities." He flashed an 'OK' sign with his hand and made a clicking sound with the corner of his mouth. "What about looks? They aren't everything but they do matter. Is she short? Tall? Pale? Tan? What else? I need to build my mental image."

"I guess she's a little tanner," I said. "She's Korean. At least her parents are. They were born there. She was born in Tampa."

"You don't say," Grandpa Kalb said and nodded his head. "I might know her grandpa."

"I highly doubt that. He doesn't live here. He's still in Korea."

"That was just a joke too. I served in the Korean War."

"Oh," I said. "I didn't even realize there was a war with Korea."

"Doesn't surprise me they gloss over it in school. But the bullets were very real, and I got the scars to prove it happened. Uncle Sam helped South Korea fight the commies in the north. When you meet her parents, you can tell them I served and even got a bronze star too. Might score you some good brownie points."

"That's never gonna happen," I said.

"Why's that?"

I wasn't about to tell him that I was running away, so I went with the reason it would be true even if I had stayed. "Her parents said she can't see me again," I said, "and she broke up with me. It's already over, even though it barely just began."

"What did I tell you last night?" Grandpa Kalb said.

Of all the things he'd told me, only one popped in my head. "If the Yankees are on, you're watching it?" I said.

"Well, yeah, I'm glad you remembered that one, but that's not what I'm talking about. What I'm talking about is Yogi. That it ain't over till it's over."

"Oh, yeah. I remember that."

"Good. Now, remember this: It's not about stating the obvious. It's not about the end being the end. It's about not quitting. It's about playing hard until the end. Because until the last out, anything can happen, as long as you don't give up."

For the first time since I'd decided to run away, the thought of actually returning home and doing whatever it took to win Grace back popped in my head. It wasn't a strong thought, I still had every intention of seeing my initial plan though, but it was a thought.

"What are you thinking about?" Grandpa Kalb asked.

"Nothing," I said. "You know. Just that you're right."

"Damn straight I am. Never forget that," Grandpa Kalb said and smiled. "I'm gonna go out on a limb and guess that your girl's parents not wanting her to see you is somehow tied into you getting suspended and possibly expelled from school, right?"

I nodded and then told Grandpa Kalb everything. I told him how Grace had gotten the marijuana for me, how I hadn't even had the chance to inhale before we were busted, and how I'd told the principal that it was mine.

"Wow," Grandpa Kalb said, leaning back in his seat as he absorbed the details. "So, you took the rap for her?"

"Yeah," I said. "Her parents would've grounded her for the rest of high school if they knew it was hers, maybe even sent her to boarding school. Mine are so busy, they'll probably forget in a couple weeks, if not sooner. I bet you think I'm an idiot, or a 'dumbass,' don't you?"

"Nope," Grandpa Kalb said. "In fact, I think the exact opposite."

"Really?" I said, taken aback.

"Yeah. I think you're in love. You weren't the first person to throw yourself on the sword of love, and you damn sure won't be the last."

"Yeah. Probably not."

"You ever hear the story about how I met your grandmother?" Grandpa Kalb asked. There was extra life in his eyes, a sparkle. Even if I had heard the story, which I hadn't, I would've said no just because of how excited he was to tell it.

"No," I said. "How'd you meet?"

"Well, it wasn't long after I'd returned from Korea. I'd just finished up my service in Annapolis and decided to visit some relatives in Baltimore before heading back to Scranton. It just so happened that your great-grandfather owned a restaurant that was down the street from my cousin's house, and your grandmother waited tables there. My cousin said they had really good pancakes, which I had been craving in Korea. So, my second day in town, I stopped by for breakfast. I know it sounds crazy saying it, but the second I laid eyes on your grandmother, I knew I wanted to marry her. She was just so beautiful. She just had an aura to her. And I wasn't the only one who noticed it. If even half the people in the place were there for the flapjacks, which were damn good, I'd be surprised. Because at least half of the people were there just to catch a glimpse of your grandmother."

"Seriously?" I said. It sounded way too ridiculous to be true.

"Damn straight," Grandpa Kalb exclaimed. "We didn't have the Internet and all these other gadgets back then. We barely had TV. I think there might have been three channels at that time and almost no one had one. So, going to a restaurant just to see a beautiful girl wasn't that far-fetched of an idea in the grand scheme of things. I knew a guy who drove two hours to buy ties from a girl he fancied."

"Wow. That is legitimately crazy."

"The line between love and crazy is as thin as they come."

"So, Grandma was your waitress that day?"

"I wish," Grandpa Kalb sighed. "Unfortunately, they put me in another waitress's section. Actually, it was your grandmother's cousin's section. Now, while Eleanor was always a sweet lady and a looker in her own right, she wasn't your grandmother."

"Okay. Then what? You just went up and talked to Grandma?"

"No," Grandpa Kalb said and scrunched his face like what I'd asked was somehow offensive. "She was hard at work. It's rude to interrupt people like that. Plus, I would've been way too nervous. I'm not good with that kind of stuff. And besides, I knew that I'd be in town for a few more days, so I decided I'd just come back the next day."

"Oh," I said. "I guess that makes sense."

"Yeah, so the next morning, I asked to be seated in her section."

"That seems kinda creepy."

"I didn't point at her and say I wanted her specific section. I just said I wanted to sit in the corner by the kitchen, which was part of her section from the day before."

"That was smart. It definitely would've been creepy otherwise."

"Exactly. You never want to be creepy. No one comes back from creepy. Of course, my move didn't work. She'd switched sections, and I got Eleanor again." Grandpa Kalb shook his head, reliving his disbelief as if it had happened just yesterday. "I'm telling you, it was déjà vu all over again, which is actually another great Yogi line."

"You realize that none of his lines make sense, right?"

"And yet, they make perfect sense," Grandpa Kalb said with a grin. "I could go on about Yogi lines for hours, but I'll save that for later. There's more to the story."

"I hope so. You still haven't even met her."

"You're paying attention. That's good," he said, smirking as he shook his finger at me. "So anyway, like the day before, I decided that I'd just talk to her the next day. Only—"

"Don't tell me the next day you both flipped sections again!"

"Exactly!" Grandpa Kalb shouted, which caught the attention of the patrons nearby. He calmed himself and continued, "This went on for a couple more days. Sometimes, I'd switch. Other times, I'd stay put. It didn't matter. Every time, I sat in the wrong damn section."

"This is ridiculous," I said, shaking my head. "It's almost getting worse than your friend with the ties."

"Believe me, I know," Grandpa Kalb agreed. "So, on my last day in Baltimore, I decided I'd stop by one more time. You know, put it in God's hands and whatever happened, happened. I go in, get seated, and what do you know ... wrong section again! I was so furious that I didn't even order anything. I just got up and stormed out."

"I would've too."

"Yeah, well, luckily your grandmother saw my little tantrum and followed me outside. She asked me what was wrong, and I told her the whole story about coming back every morning and switching sections."

"How'd you come back from creepy?"

"By the grace of God. Believe it or not, she'd been switching sections so that she could talk to me."

"No way."

"If I was lying, you wouldn't be here."

"True."

"As soon as she went on break, we had our first date. We split a milkshake in the back alley of the restaurant."

"That sounds romantic," I said sarcastically.

"Hey! It was. I was so ecstatic that I didn't even notice the smells. An hour later, I hopped on the train back to Scranton. I swear I smiled the whole damn ride home."

"Then what happened?" I asked. I'd never really heard anything about their relationship and the whole crazy introduction had sucked me in like a mystery on Investigation Discovery.

"We wrote letters long distance for about a month, and then I proposed."

"After ONE month?" I said, my eyes going wide. It wasn't much longer than Grace and I had been talking.

"It wasn't fast for back then," Grandpa Kalb said. "This will probably blow your mind too, but I didn't even have an engagement ring when I proposed either."

"Why not?"

"I mean, why don't you buy a baseball franchise?"

"Because I don't want one."

"Well, assuming you did."

"I can't afford one."

"Bingo," Grandpa Kalb said. "Same reason I didn't get a ring. We were only engaged for a month before we got married. After that, we never spent more than ten hours apart until the day she died." Grandpa Kalb choked up at the end, and his eyes began to tear in the creases. I handed him a napkin from the dispenser on the table. "Thanks," he said with a sniffle, taking the napkin and using it to dab his tears and then blew his nose. "I know it sounds too good to be true, but that's just how it is sometimes with life ... and with baseball, miracles happen. Yep, if it's meant to be, you'll get Grace back. Then one day, you'll get to tell your grandkids about how you took the rap for her. It might not sound like the best story now, but with the way this country's going, you never know. In fifty years, that might actually qualify for romantic."

"Ha," I chuckled. "Yeah. You never know? Who would've thought drinking milkshakes in an alley would?"

"Exactly. Every couple has their story." Grandpa Kalb smiled as he reminisced.

"Uncle Herschel's Favorite," said our waitress as she laid Grandpa Kalb's plate on the tables, the clanging waking Grandpa Kalb from his daydreaming.

"Oh, thanks," he said.

"And one delicious but not-quite-as-delicious-as-Waffle-House waffle."

"Thanks," I said with a smile as she handed me my plate.

"Enjoy," she said and headed off.

I immediately tore into my waffle, which was still really good.

Grandpa Kalb took one bite of his catfish and then stopped. "I just had an idea."

"What's that?" I asked with a mouthful of waffle and lips sticky with syrup.

"Well, I still feel bad about tricking you. So, what if I got a real disguise? What if I went goth?"

"Really?" I said, almost spitting out my food. "That would be hilarious."

"I'm not talking about any of that makeup or painting my nails kind of stuff," Grandpa Kalb was quick to add. "Just dying my hair and getting all black clothes."

"It'd definitely make you look different. People your age usually look pretty weird when they dye their hair."

"I know. It looks completely ridiculous. That's why I've never done it. But with the black hair and clothes ... I'd also kinda look a little like Johnny Cash. The Man in Black."

I looked at my grandpa, trying to imagine the comparison. "I don't remember him being so bald on top."

"He wasn't. That's why I said kinda. I'm obviously not the spitting image."

I grinned. I was just messing with him, returning the favor for his Forrest Gump joke.

"Ah, I see what you did there," Grandpa Kalb said as he nodded his head. "So, what do you think?"

I thought—or I should say that I knew—that it wouldn't make us even; but, at the very least, it was another step in the right direction. "I think it could be cool."

"Perfect," Grandpa Kalb said. "Then let's do it!" He smirked and wiggled his eyebrows.

15

Once we'd finished our lunches and split the baked apple dumplin' dessert, we made a stop at the nearby Florence Food Lion and picked up a Just For Men hair dying kit. Grandpa Kalb was adamant about needing something "for men," even though I'd informed him that Grace had told me that the women's products were actually superior.

After that, we crossed the parking lot to the Goodwill. Much to my disappointment, the clothes they had in my size were just as bad or worse than the ones my grandpa had gotten. After coming to terms with the fact that I was stuck with my Forrest Gump gear, I helped Grandpa Kalb pick out his new look. I kept it simple: black jeans and a black long-sleeved button-down shirt. As we headed to the car, Grandpa Kalb made at least three Johnny Cash references that I caught and, most likely, a few more that I didn't.

"I think we're good on the Johnny Cash stuff," I said as I started the engine.

"The name is Charlie Cash," Grandpa Kalb said as he ran a comb through his hair.

"Where did you get that comb?" I asked, having never seen him with it.

"I found it in my new pants," he said with a grin as he patted his pants pocket.

I cringed. "Ugh. Seriously? That's disgusting."

"Everybody knows that Charlie Cash likes to walk the line."

"What line is that? The line between unhygienic and incredibly unhygienic?"

"It's still a line. And Charlie Cash is right down the middle."

I just shook my head. Thankfully, that was the last I heard of Charlie Cash and his ways.

We hopped back on the highway, but only for about twenty minutes because Grandpa Kalb demanded that we stop at this roadside attraction on the southern border of North and South Carolina, which was aptly named South of the Border. We'd seen the signs advertising it for over an hour, and he needed to "see what the fuss was about." Apparently, it'd started as a place to sell alcohol to the dry counties just across the state line in North Carolina and then grew into this crazy Mexican-themed wonderland where they peddled fireworks and marginal food, and where every worker went by the name Pedro. While I imagine it was packed during the summer months, on a Friday afternoon at the end of September, the "fuss" was downright depressing. It was just a bunch of Pedros and us. Grandpa Kalb bought a pack of bottle rockets because he felt bad, and then we took off.

As we made our way through North Carolina, Grandpa Kalb was more determined than ever to convince me of the brilliance of Yogi Berra and rattled off some of his sayings. His plan started off poorly because the lines he kept picking were more confusing than anything else.

"I don't get it," I said. "How could it get late early?"

Grandpa Kalb sighed in frustration. "It didn't actually get late," he said. "It was probably just getting dark outside earlier because they were further south or something. Either way, you're overthinking it. You're not supposed to overthink Yogi-isms. You just enjoy them."

"Fine. Give me another one."

"Okay," he said and then thought for a few seconds. "Here's one. The game is 90% mental. The other half is physical." He must have seen the gears in my head had started to turn, because he quickly shouted, "Don't think! Just enjoy it."

"I am," I said, chuckling at him more than the line, which was actually pretty funny.

"Good. Here's another classic. Yogi was asked if he went to this particular restaurant, and he said, 'Nobody goes there anymore, it's too crowded.'"

"Ha!" I blurted out. "Okay. That is pretty good."

"You bet your ass it is! They all are." Grandpa Kalb stroked his chin for a second and then smirked. "All right. This is the best one yet, and the most fitting, since we're traveling ourselves. So, the team was on a road trip, and someone told Yogi, who was the manager at the time, that he thought they were lost. And Yogi said—" Grandpa Kalb started to giggle.

He tried to continue, but his giggle only grew and kept him from finishing getting past the first two words. He tried to recollect himself and start again. But Grandpa Kalb only got one word out before he exploded in an uncontrollable fit, laughing so hard that his eyes began to well up.

"Oh, my god. You're crying," I said, laughing myself. "Are you gonna be all right?"

Grandpa Kalb nodded in between outbursts. He closed his

eyes, covered his mouth with his fist, and then took a deep breath through his nose to calm himself down.

"Am I ever gonna find out what Yogi said?" I asked.

Grandpa Kalb nodded, took a couple of smaller breaths, and then, with his eyes still closed and his arms extended as if to steady himself, said, "Yogi said, 'Yeah, but we're making great time.'" No sooner had the last word left his mouth than he blew up again.

I couldn't help but lose it myself, equally amused by my grandpa and the wit of Yogi Berra.

"They were lost, but they were making good time," Grandpa Kalb squealed, his damp eyes bursting with tears that streamed down his cheeks.

"That's definitely my favorite so far," I said as my body shook with amusement.

"It's up there with his best," Grandpa Kalb said and grabbed his side. "It gets me every time."

"That's an understatement." I took a deep breath and let the last of my giggles go. I noticed my grandpa was still clutching his ribs. "You better be careful. You're gonna hurt yourself."

"I'm fine. It's just a cramp," he said and then took a long wheezing breath. After a few more high-pitched squeals snuck out, he regained his composure. "Oh, man, that was great."

"It sure was," I agreed.

The song on the radio, which had been turned down, switched and caught Grandpa Kalb's attention. "Speaking of great," he said and then cranked the knob to turn up the volume, "this song is right up there with that quote."

I'd never heard the song or singer before, but I was fairly certain, based on Grandpa Kalb's enthusiastic reaction, that it was his pal Frank Sinatra. "Come on," I insisted, "we have a good thing going here. Let's not ruin it with Sinatra."

"You can't ruin anything with Sinatra. Especially this song. This is 'My Way.'"

"Great," I groaned, misinterpreting what he meant, "I thought you were done bossing me around."

"That's the name of the song. Just give the real Frank a chance, a clean slate. If you never want to hear another Sinatra song after 'My Way,' that's fine by me."

"All right," I conceded. "But if this song sucks, I get to control the radio for the rest of the day."

"Deal," Grandpa Kalb said and put out his hand so we could shake on it.

Sinatra started off singing something sappy about the end being near and curtain calls. It was slow and depressing and not really doing anything for me for the first minute or so.

"I don't know," I said. "It's already losing me."

"Just hold your damn horses," Grandpa Kalb said. "It's about to pick up."

By "about to" he really meant not for another thirty seconds. That was when the horns kicked in, and Grandpa Kalb started to sing along with the chorus, waving his arms emphatically as he pretended to orchestrate the band.

After the chorus, the song slowed back down and so did Grandpa Kalb's hand gestures. "Still losing you?" he asked and winked as if there was no way it could still be true.

"Eh," I said swaying my head side to side, "it's getting better."

"Well, just wait for the grand finale. That's when it will really get'cha."

"Oh, I can't wait."

"Sarcasm! I know how that works."

The song picked back up for the finale and so did Grandpa Kalb's flourishing fingers. This time, he looked at me while he sang. I made sure to keep my eyes mostly on the road—since I knew he would remind me to if I didn't—and grinned as I watched him with my peripheral vision.

Grandpa Kalb switched to acting out the lyrics as he sang, including clenching his fists and throwing a few air jabs when the song talked about taking blows, before belting out, "MY WAY!"

As the music built to its final crescendo, Grandpa Kalb shook me by the shoulder and shouted, "See, we're just like Frank! We're going to Yankee Stadium, and we're doing it our way!" He closed out the song like any good conductor would, and then turned the radio back down and asked, "All right, give it to me, honest opinion?"

"Honest opinion?" I said. "It wasn't that bad. I guess it was okay."

"Okay?" He nodded his head for a moment, considering whether to accept it or not. "I'm gonna take that. I'll take it!"

I chuckled at how thrilled he was by my tepid response. "I will say this, I do think you're a way better singer than your friend Art. That's for sure."

"Why thank you," he said smiling from ear to ear. "Of course, my voice is like two alley cats fighting over a mouse compared to your grandmother's. She could put Doris Day to shame."

"I've never heard alley cats fight or Doris Day, but I'm assuming the former is bad and the latter is good."

"Bingo!"

A few seconds passed, and then I said, "I have a question." There was something that had been running through my mind since before we'd even left on our trip, but Grandpa Kalb and I had spent so much time arguing that I hadn't had the chance, nor really cared, to inquire about it until that moment.

"Ask away," Grandpa Kalb said.

"So, I understand how you really like the team and the players, but what's so special about Yankee Stadium?"

"On a superficial level? Nothing. Just read any paper and they'll tell you how old and outdated it is. It's just a hunk of concrete, metal, and plastic. But what makes it special, is the same thing that makes anything special—all the memories. Take a guess where your grandmother and I took our honeymoon?

"I don't know. Hawaii?"

"No," Grandpa Kalb exclaimed and looked at me as if I'd given the most outrageous answer ever. "Why the hell would you guess Hawaii?"

"I don't know. That's where my parents went. Don't a lot of people go there?"

"Yeah. I mean, they do now. But not back in 1954. Plus, your grandmother didn't like flying. Actually, she was too afraid to fly to find out if she did or didn't like flying. But either way, we were just talking about Yankee Stadium and memories."

"Wait. You seriously went to Yankee Stadium for your honeymoon?"

"Damn straight! At the time it was the nicest thing we could afford. We even splurged and sat about twenty rows behind home plate. There was a nice usher too, and he let us stand on the stairs just behind the netting after we told him it was our honeymoon."

"Nice."

"Yep. Outside of meeting your grandmother, our wedding, and your mother's birth, pretty much all of my best and biggest memories took place at Yankee Stadium. My last memories of my father and my older brother also took place at The Big House." He gazed out the window and sniffled. While many years had passed between those memories and that moment, they clearly still struck an emotional cord. "Dad always loved the nosebleeds. And Edward and I snuck in through the outfield for old times' sake just before he left for Navy boot camp. We just walked around and watched the game from all over the stadium."

"What happened to them, Edward and great-grandpa Kalb?" I asked. My mom had never really talked much about her uncle or her grandpa, and I had never really made an effort to ask. I actually didn't even know Grandpa Kalb had a brother.

"My father died when I was ten, he was trying to rescue his friends after their coal mine collapsed, and Edward was one of the many brave soldiers that never made it back from Normandy. Yogi was at D-Day too. He was a gunner's mate, just like Edward. Although, he obviously came back. I like to think that he and Edward were buddies."

"I didn't know any of that. About your dad, Edward, or Yogi."

"Yep. Dad was thirty-six and Edward was barely eighteen. By the time I was your age, I was already the man of the house." He wiped a tear from the corner of his eye and smiled through the pain. "But it's not all sad memories. Most of my memories from Yankee Stadium were pretty damn amazing."

"What's the best one?" I asked, hoping to cheer him up with better thoughts.

"Well, your grandmother would be livid if I didn't say our honeymoon."

"Okay. Second best."

"That's easy. Game six of the 1977 World Series. That was the game where Reggie Jackson knocked three tatters out of the park. I took your mother to that game. It was her eleventh birthday present. The stadium was sheer madness. Usually, we sat in the outfield bleachers, but this time we were right on the baseline, front row. I'd gotten the tickets as a gift from my boss for not missing a day of work in fifteen years."

"Wow. That's really impressive."

"That's nothing. I didn't miss a day of work my whole career. My co-workers called me the Iron Horse. That's a Lou Gehrig reference. Although, his real name was actually Henry Louis Gehrig, which is why I tried to get your parents to name you Henry, so you'd be Henry Lewis. Unfortunately, your dad had an uncle named Henry Lewis who was a mess, so that was off the table. Anyway, back to the game. The Yankees were up 3-2 in the series, so a win meant another championship. By the time the game was down to the last out, half of the stadium was sitting on the edge of the fence, just waiting to run the field. You can't get away with that kind of stuff nowadays; you'd get tased. But not back then, they didn't even have tasers. Just a bunch of Barney Fife's trying to protect the field. They announced that they'd quadrupled the security forces, but that didn't scare anyone. As soon as the Yankees got the last out, a bunt pop-up to the pitcher, it was like the dam broke, and this massive wave of people rushed onto the field, including your mother and me."

"No way!" I said. "She would never do anything crazy like that."

"Oh, she did," he said. "And it gets even better. So, everyone was going nuts on the field, and, understandably, Reggie Jackson wanted nothing to do with this mob celebration. So he charges toward the dugout like a goddamn bull in Pamplona, Spain, weaving through the crowd and tossing anyone and everyone out of his way. Now, your mother got away from me a little, just like ten feet. Not too far. But I see she's right in Reggie's path, and he's still charging hard."

"Oh, no," I said, envisioning Reggie Jackson chucking my mom.

"Oh, yes," Grandpa Kalb said with a nod. "So, I push my way through the crowd and get to her just in time to move her out of the way. I look eye-to-eye with Mr. October himself for the splittest of split seconds before he flings me like a sack of potatoes. I swear I went eight feet in the air and landed hard on my side. As I'm lying on the grass, which was easily the nicest grass I've ever laid on, and I'll never forget the sweet smell, I hear your mother yell, 'Hey, Reggie, that wasn't very nice!'" Grandpa Kalb chuckled at the memory.

"Now that sounds like my mom," I said with a chuckle of my own. "And she did have a point. That sounded painful."

"It was. I never went to the doctor, but I swear I broke at least a rib, if not two or three. I still showed up to work the next day on-time, even though the whole right side of my body was almost as dark as this shirt. To add insult to injury, the video of the whole thing was all over the news. My friends gave me hell about it for years. I guess you could say that was my fifteen minutes of fame."

"And shame."

"Ha! More shame than fame, that's for sure. Yep. Now they're just gonna tear down the stadium for something new and flashy, and they're gonna tear down all the history and memories—like your mother and I on the field after game six—with it."

"Well, at least it's on video," I said. "That means it's probably on YouTube."

"What's a you tube?" Grandpa asked, his face perking up a bit. "I don't have a tube."

"That's just the name. It's a website. They have almost every video ever recorded. If our hotel tonight has the Internet or a business center, we can check it out and see if it's online. I feel like it has to be."

"That would be great." Grandpa Kalb smiled. "How about we drive for another hour and a half or so and then call it a day. After all"—he started to giggle—"we're making good time."

I shook my head and grinned. "Yeah, we are. And we're not even lost."

16

"Damn!" I said as I giddily watched the YouTube clip of Grandpa Kalb—a much slimmer, thicker-haired, 1970s version of him—getting tossed by Reggie Jackson on the tiny computer monitor. It was one of two computers in the equally undersized business center at the Courtyard Marriott just outside of Rocky Mount, North Carolina. I sat in the lone desk chair while my grandpa hovered over my shoulder.

"What did I tell you?" he said.

"I don't know about eight feet, but you're right about the sack of potatoes part."

"Yeah, well, it sure as hell felt like eight feet. My bones ache just watching it."

"Then you might want to turn away," I said with a grin, "because I gotta watch it again."

"Nah, I'll be fine," he said, smiling. "Some things are worth the pain."

I replayed the clip of Grandpa Kalb getting steamrolled a few more times. While he'd definitely exaggerated the height that he was thrown, the rest of his story was spot on, everything from the fans waiting on the fence to the swarming of the field to my mom almost getting run over by Reggie. You could see it all. If anything, it was even wilder than I'd imagined. It didn't seem like reality. It seemed like it was from a movie where there was some crazed hippie prison riot or something. The whole stadium, all fifty-thousand-plus people, took part in the pandemonium.

I shook my head in disbelief as I finished watching the video one last time. "Man, that really was insane with everyone on the field. What was it like?"

"Unbelievable," Grandpa Kalb said. "There was an energy. A feeling. You can't really put it into words. People who didn't know each other from Adam were hugging and high-fiving. You really had to be there to understand it. I'll tell you one thing, if you were at that game, there's no way you would ever say that baseball was boring."

"Yeah. I mean, I don't actually think it is boring. I was just trying to get under your skin."

"Really?" Grandpa Kalb said, stretching out each syllable. "I never would've guessed that."

"To be honest, this is probably the most baseball that I've ever watched."

Grandpa Kalb snorted derisively. "I consider that a failure on the part of your mother and father. And while I take no credit for your soccer-loving father, I raised your mother a lot better than that."

I chuckled.

Grandpa Kalb didn't. "I'm serious," he said, his face matching his words.

"Well, I actually think it seems like a pretty cool sport," I conceded

"Huh?" Grandpa Kalb said, squinting his eyes and cupping his ear with his hand. "My hearing sometimes comes and goes."

"I said it looks like a pretty cool sport," I said, raising my voice.

"Still didn't quite catch that," he said, raising his voice too.

"I said—" I stopped as soon as I noticed the smirk appearing on Grandpa Kalb's face.

"Gotcha!" he exclaimed and shook me by the shoulders, his grin growing with each shake. "I just wanted to hear you say it a couple of times. I knew you'd eventually come along."

"Why do I always fall for your crap?" I said and shook my head.

"Because I'm good," he said. "Plain and simple." His veneer vanished when his eyes locked on the computer's clock. "Hot damn! The game is about to start. What do you say we head up to the room, and I teach you some of the ins and out of America's pastime and the best team in the history of the sport? Or any sport, for that matter."

"Why not?" I said with a shrug and stood up from the chair.

"Perfect," Grandpa Kalb said and then threw his arm around me.

As we headed up to our room, Grandpa Kalb explained why The Bronx Bombers—one of the nicknames for the Yankees—were "objectively speaking" the best team ever. While I found his self-proclaimed objectivity laughable at first, he had the stats to back it up. The most convincing stat he cited was the Yankees 26 World Series titles, which were 16 more than the next closest team, the St. Louis Cardinals. In fact, the next closest title-winning team, in any sport, was the Boston Celtics, whose 16 NBA championships were still ten shy of the Yankees' total. Of course, bringing up Boston led to a mini-tirade by Grandpa Kalb about the Red Sox, who had won their seventh World Series the year before and had broken the Curse of the Bambino—an 86-year title drought, set off by the Sox selling Babe Ruth to the Yankees—just a few years before that.

By the time we made it to the room and found the game on the TV, the Yankees had just started running onto the field. Grandpa Kalb explained that since it was a home game for the Yankees, they had to bat second in the "bottom" of the inning. While the Orioles, the away team, hit first in the "top" of the inning. The whole top and bottom part didn't make much sense to me, but Grandpa Kalb said it made more sense when I saw the scoreboard since it was divided into frames with the away team on the top and home team on the bottom.

A graphic image of the field and the players assigned positions flashed on the field.

"First thing's first," Grandpa Kalb said as he excitedly rubbed his hands together.

"Is that another Yogi line?" I asked.

"No. But it kinda sounds like it could be, right?" I nodded, and Grandpa Kalb continued, "Since this is your first real Yankees experience, you have an incredibly important decision to make."

"Really?" I said, surprised that things were moving so fast. "Already?"

"Yep. It's something you have to do, and it's gonna play a big role in your future as a fan. You need to pick your favorite player."

"Why?"

"Because everyone has a favorite player."

"But I don't even know any of them."

"It doesn't matter. Just pick one."

"Okay." I scanned the names on the screen, one of which was highlighted. "Is Alex Rodriguez any good?"

"Yeah, of course. He's an MVP winner, but don't pick him. You want someone homegrown, someone who came up through the farm system?"

"The 'farm system?' Am I gonna have to learn a lot about agriculture to understand any of this?"

Grandpa Kalb shook his head at my terrible joke. "That's just what they call their minor league teams," he said. "A-Rod signed as a free agent. I'll explain it more later."

"Fine. How about Derek Jeter? Is he any good?"

"Uh, yeah. He's an amazing player. The face of the franchise, the best Yankee of your generation, and a future first-ballot Hall of Famer. But, he's already everyone's favorite. And you're not a conformist, right?" Grandpa Kalb grinned, clearly getting a kick out of throwing one of my lines back at me. "Come on, one more shot."

"All right. Last choice ... Robinson Cano."

"Now, that is a great pick," he said. "Young guy. Tons of talent. Heck of a player."

Grandpa Kalb proceeded to tell me everything he knew about Robinson Cano: his age, hometown, how he batted, how he threw, how his parents had named him after Jackie Robinson, where he hit in the order, where he could eventually hit in the order, and so on and so on. I was starting to think he might keep rattling off random information on Robinson for the rest of the game, when the Orioles scored a run and Grandpa Kalb finally changed gears.

"Dammit!" he shouted and then quickly backtracked. "Don't worry. That's nothing. We'll get it back. Just wait until the bottom of the inning. We'll get it back."

In the bottom of the inning, the Yankees didn't get it back. All three of the hitters went down in order, which Grandpa Kalb informed me was called a 1-2-3 inning.

In the top of the second inning, the Orioles scored another run to go up 2-0.

"We better get that back too," I said.

"We will, and then some," Grandpa Kalb said confidently. "All it takes is a base hit and then a hanging curve and we're back even. Besides, we still have twenty-four of our twenty-seven outs left. Plenty of time. Just watch what we do in the second."

"We" did nothing in the bottom of the second and neither did the Yankees. They got a hit but then the Orioles made a couple lighting quick throws to pull off a double play or "turn two." The nifty play didn't get Grandpa Kalb down. He just kept up his mantra that the next inning was going to be our inning.

The top of the third started off better than the two innings before. Instead of giving up another hit to the leadoff batter, and then giving up runs, the Yankees pitcher was able to get a 1-2-3 inning of his own.

"That's what we needed!" Grandpa Kalb shouted and jumped up from his seat on the edge of the bed as the first baseman caught the final out of the inning. "Retired the side. Three up and three down. That'll give us a spark." He patted me on the shoulder and grinned. "And now your favorite player is leading things off."

After the commercial break, Cano stepped to the plate.

"Let's see what Robbie can do," Grandpa Kalb said as he sat back down on the bed next to me and then shouted at the TV through cupped hands, "Come on, Cano! Hit one out for your new biggest fan."

Full disclosure, I definitely didn't feel like Cano's new biggest fan, or even much of a fan at all. Leading up to his at bat, I had hardly been into the game. Even when he took his practice cuts and then stepped into the batter's box, it didn't exactly move the needle. However, after Cano got set, and the pitcher went into his windup, a little voice in my head quietly began cheering, "Come on." And as the ball left the pitcher's hand, I could feel my heart thump in my chest a little louder than before. It thumped even harder as the ball landed in the catcher's mitt with a pop.

"Good eye," Grandpa Kalb said as Cano watched the pitch, which the umpire called a ball. He turned to me and patted me on the back. "He knows the strike zone as well as anyone."

I nodded, only then realizing that I'd been holding my breath. I exhaled and turned back to the TV. My heart continued to pick up, along with the voice in my head. "You can do this Cano," it said. Another voice chimed in, "What are you doing? Why do you even care?" The first voice quickly snapped back, "Quiet!" My voice of reason or doubt or whatever you want to call it listened, staying silent for the next two pitches, both of which were balls.

"3-0," Grandpa Kalb exclaimed. "He's gotta take this. Rarely do you swing at 3-0."

This wasn't one of those rare times. Cano watched the pitch all the way into the catcher's mitt, a perfect strike. Cano didn't watch the fifth pitch; he fouled it off for strike two.

"Now it's getting interesting," Grandpa Kalb said as he tapped his fingers together and wiggled his eyebrows excitedly. "Full count. What's he gonna do?"

My heart was beating so fast and heavy that I could feel it in the back of my throat. Part of me just wanted it to be over. The other part of me, including the voice in my head, was screaming, "Crush it!"

That's exactly what Cano did. As soon as I heard the thundering crack of the bat meeting the ball, I knew that it was unlike any of the hits from earlier in the game. The ball sailed into the right field bleachers, and Grandpa Kalb and I both leaped from the bed and executed the worst high-five ever. He hit me in the forearm, and then my arm slapped his shoulder. We didn't care though. We just kept jumping up and down.

"Robbie Cano, don't cha know!" Grandpa Kalb screamed.

"He destroyed that!" I shouted.

"Yeah, he did!" Grandpa Kalb quickly lost steam and hunched over to catch his breath. "I told you we'd get it back. Now, it's time to get a rally going. If only we had rally caps."

"What's a rally cap?"

"It's a regular hat, but you turn it inside out and wear it. It helps the team rally. Usually, people save it for the last inning, but I like to do it whenever I get the urge for a rally."

"And that actually works?"

"Well, yeah. Some of the time. Like maybe 20% of the time."

"That's not very good," I said.

"Even the best hitters fail seven out of ten times. And it's better than none of the time."

I couldn't argue with that logic. Nor was I planning to, when an idea popped into my head. "What about rally shirts?"

"Hmmm," Grandpa Kalb said, tapping his chin as he gave my plan serious consideration. "I've never done a rally shirt before. But it just might work."

"Then let's do it," I said.

"Rally shirts it is!" Grandpa Kalb screamed as he struggled to work his way out of his button-down without bothering to unbutton it.

I had just finished pulling my last arm through my inside-out shirt when the next batter laced a single to left field.

"It's already working," Grandpa Kalb said as he poked his head through his flipped shirt.

A couple pitches and a stolen base later, Brett Gardner smoked a double, and the game was tied. Grandpa Kalb and I celebrated. This time, we took a second to coordinate the logistics of our high-five, so it was less awkward and so our palms actually met.

"We're back even," Grandpa Kalb exclaimed. "Damn! I should've been using rally shirts my whole life."

The next two innings were full of tension. Both teams had scoring chances, and both teams barely escaped their respective jams. Then, in the bottom of the fifth, the Yankees got two singles and a stolen base to have first and third with one out. After a fly ball out of bounds to the third baseman, it appeared that the Yankees were going to squander this chance too. But with a 2-1 count, the Orioles pitcher threw a wild pitch, and the Yankees jumped ahead for the first time in the game.

The Orioles almost put something together in the sixth but went down in order in the seventh and the eighth. In the top of the ninth, the bullpen doors in the outfield opened up and Mariano Rivera, or Sandman as Grandpa Kalb said he was called, jogged toward the mound with his head down while Metallica's "Enter Sandman" played.

"This is pretty badass," I said, nodding my head to the music.

"Yeah, well, Mariano is pretty badass himself," Grandpa Kalb said.

While Rivera reinforced my grandpa's confidence with the

first two batters, getting two quick outs, the third batter singled and then the fourth batter reached on a slow roller back to the mound that he barely beat out.

"Come on! He was out," Grandpa Kalb shouted, just before they showed the replay proving that the runner was safe. "Well, at least he should've been."

"Maybe we should switch back to regular shirts," I said, afraid that I'd be our undoing.

"Nonsense. The rally shirts got us this far. We gotta roll with them to rally out of this jam. Besides, they call it a closer for a reason, and Mariano is one of the best ever."

"Then why did he give up those two hits?"

"Because he's human. And just like every other human, there are times when he isn't at his best, when he doesn't have his best stuff to work with. What separates the good from the great is the ability to make it work when you don't have your best stuff."

I nodded and then we both turned back to the TV. We held our breaths, our hands clenched tight and our butts barely hanging on the edge of the bed. Fortunately, we didn't need to wait long to get our relief. On Rivera's next pitch, he got the batter to pop up to the catcher.

"That's the ball game!" Grandpa Kalb exclaimed as the ball landed in the catcher's mitt.

"Wow," I said, letting out a deep sigh of relief. "I'm glad that's over. That was too close."

"The best ones always are. Now, we just need to hope that the Blue Jays can come back on the Red Sox. So we can keep that tragic number from shrinking."

"What's a tragic number?"

"It's the opposite of a magic number, which is part of your next lesson in baseball, along with a little lesson on the art of pitch framing and an introduction to a group of fine individuals affectionately known as the Bleacher Creatures. But before we get into any of that, we have some very important business to take care of." He smirked and shot me a knowing wink like I was in on his business plan.

Of course, I had no idea what he was referring to or what we had to "take care of."

17

The next morning, I was jolted awake. This time, it wasn't from a sudden burst of sunlight but from setting my groggy, half-opened eyes on the dark-haired stranger in the adjacent bed. My eyelids shot open so fast that I swear they broke the sound barrier.

I racked my brain, trying to figure out who it might be and what I should do. I couldn't decide if I should fight or flee. I also didn't know what had happened to my grandpa. Before I could come to a decision on a plan, the stranger rolled over, and I realized that it was my grandpa.

The clouds covering my foggy morning memory dissipated, and I remembered Grandpa Kalb's "important business" from the night before. I didn't think it was that important—it was just dying his hair with the Just For Men kit—and I'd even given him a chance to back out of the deal. However, my grandpa insisted on going through with it, explaining, "Charlie Kalb doesn't welsh on a bet or go back on his word."

Relieved that I hadn't ended up in some random person's room, I sighed and gently closed my eyes. A few seconds later, my eyes burst back open as I was startled by what sounded like some wild animals getting slaughtered. Really, it was just Grandpa Kalb again, snoring himself awake.

I'd never heard anything like it. First came the snore, which was followed by a violent, gagging cough. It all concluded with some gum slapping and then about ten seconds of incoherent mumbling.

A few seconds after the mumbling stopped, Grandpa Kalb yawned and then rolled onto his side to find me staring at him. "Great. You're already up."

"Yeah," I said, "I don't think anyone could sleep through that crazy noise you just made."

Grandpa Kalb slid his legs over the edge of his bed and slowly sat up. "Sorry about that. Just another perk of getting old. Noises and hair growing everywhere."

"Can't wait," I said and glanced at the clock. It was already after seven. "Looks like we both lost our worms to the early bird today."

"Shit," Grandpa Kalb said, matching my gaze. "Thankfully, this place has a decent Continental breakfast. We need to grab a quick bite and then skedaddle. I need to get to Baltimore ASAP so I can do a few things."

"Works for me," I said as I rolled out of bed. "I was just gonna take a quick shower, but I should be good to go in five minutes."

"Perfect."

My shower should've been shorter than even I had intended, since my new haircut didn't really require much care. However, as I rubbed my fingers across the stubbly hairs, I was reminded of what was previously there. That inevitably led to thoughts of

Grace, which then spurred more thoughts, thoughts of ditching my plan to run away.

Unlike the first time, these thoughts weren't fleeting. This time, they stuck. Maybe my grandpa was right and that maybe I shouldn't just give up. Maybe ... it wasn't over until it was over. I could just go to the game, head back to Florida with my grandpa, and then do whatever it took to win Grace back.

The more I thought about it, the more I liked the idea. Even though I wasn't fully committed to bailing on my plan just yet, my mind decided to move onto working on ideas for what I could do to win Grace back. My mind cycled through everything from flowers and a card to one of those airplane signs to standing outside of her house with a boombox.

The boombox idea was probably the best one I'd had up to that point. It was a move from *Say Anything*, which was one of Grace's favorite movies. She had a thing for '80s movies, especially ones that starred John Cusack or Molly Ringwald. I think it was because a lot of the movies were about teens discovering who they really were, beyond all the stereotypes placed on them.

It wasn't until the water turned suddenly hot that I was woken from my plotting daydreams. I shut off the shower and grabbed a towel. As I dried off, I realized that I hadn't heard anything from my grandpa, which seemed off since I knew my shower had run long and that he was in a hurry. I quickly finished toweling off and then threw on a fresh pair of boxers.

When I returned to the room, Grandpa Kalb was still sitting on the corner of his bed and rubbing his eyes. "Everything all right?" I asked.

"Yeah," he said. "I'm just not used to late nights like last night anymore."

It had been a long night, even for me. While we'd waited for his hair dye set in, Grandpa Kalb had given me a master's course lesson on baseball. After that, we stayed up till nearly one in the morning watching game highlights on ESPN while Grandpa Kalb pointed out some of the little intricacies of the game that the announcers—who, according to my grandpa, were more interested in their "dumbass catchphrases"—had glossed over.

"Me either," I said, yawning as I threw on my shorts.

Grandpa Kalb stood up and wobbled to his suitcase to retrieve his pillbox.

As I buttoned my shirt, I watched him pluck a handful of pills and then put about half of them back in his container. He was about to throw them all in his mouth when he stopped, his cupped palm an inch away. He turned his gaze up toward me, a suspicious look in his eye that bordered on paranoia.

"Why the hell are you watching me so closely?" he snapped.

"Sorry," I said, momentarily averting my eyes. "It's just a lot of pills."

His face flattened and so did the tone of his voice. "Yeah, it sure is. You can add that to the noises and hair. When you get old, you get to take a pill for everything."

"What are they all for?"

"I'm not sure I can even remember," Grandpa Kalb said and shook his head. He went through the pills in his palm, holding each one up while he described its purpose. "This is for my heart. This is for my blood pressure. This is for my liver. This is to make sure my liver pill doesn't affect my heart pill. This is just a multivitamin, Centrum Silver, I think. And this last one ... I'm not sure what it is. Oh, yeah. It's B12, which, coincidentally, is supposed to help my memory."

"What about the ones you put back?"

Grandpa Kalb's glare returned briefly and then disappeared

again. He took a second to respond. "They're just more of the same. Some days the doses are different. But hey, I'm not a doctor, I just do what they tell me to do."

"What about the shot you take?"

"That's insulin. For my diabetes."

I noticed a small orange prescription bottle that was by itself on the bottom of the pillbox. "And what's that?"

"I don't take that," Grandpa Kalb said, both quickly and adamantly.

"Why not?" I said, confused why it was such a big deal to him. "What's it for?"

"What the hell is this, twenty questions? I said I don't take it."

"Sorry," I said, throwing my hands up. "I didn't realize it was such a sensitive subject. Forget I asked." I went back to getting dressed.

A few seconds later, I heard Grandpa Kalb sigh. "I'm sorry for blowing my lid," he said. "The pills are something called Marinol. It's for my glaucoma."

"I feel like I've heard of that before."

"Yeah, well, your pot smoking friends probably talk about it a lot. It's synthetic THC. But like I said, I don't take it."

"Why not? Everyone says it's supposed to help. I mean, whenever they talk about medicinal marijuana, they always mention glaucoma."

"I don't take it because … well … everyone knows marijuana is a gateway drug. It leads to harder stuff. Plus, whenever they ask you if you do any drugs, I don't want to have to say yes."

I took a moment to try to get a read on my grandpa. Even though his response sounded completely genuine, what he'd said was so incredibly absurd that I couldn't tell if he was kidding or not. Before I could decide one way or the other, I was overcome by the ridiculousness of his response and started to crack up.

"What's so funny?" Grandpa Kalb said, surprisingly self-conscious.

"You," I said, still laughing. "Your excuse. I mean, that's hilarious. One, it's not gonna lead to harder drugs unless you just want to do harder drugs. That's a bigger myth than the rising fastball you were telling me about. And two, who's even asking you if you do drugs?"

"I get asked that a lot," he said, getting defensive.

"By who? It's not like you're applying for jobs."

"Well, mostly doctors, when I'm filling out forms."

"You mean the same doctors that prescribed it to you. I'm pretty sure they aren't going to judge you. Wow!" I said and shook my head. "You're such a tight-ass. But now I know where my mom gets it from."

Grandpa Kalb stewed for a second. He looked like he wanted to respond, and harshly; but instead, he just silently filled his syringe halfway, emptied it into his abdomen, and then put back in his pillbox and packed the pillbox away.

"I'm sorry," I said as I let out the last of my little chuckles, "but that's just too damn funny."

GRANDPA KALB hardly said a word while we loaded up on the Continental breakfast, which consisted of a random assortment of pastries and few tiny boxes of cereal, or for our first hour back on the highway. I tried to get the conversation going a couple of times, but all I could get out of him was a nod or a "yeah." So, after my third failed attempt to spark a conversation, I just gave up and decided to see how long he could hold out.

I was pretty sure he wasn't talking because he was mad that I laughed at him. It seemed like a pretty weak reason to get so upset. At least, that's what I told myself. It's also why I wasn't in a rush to apologize. However, I realized pretty quickly that it was a lot easier to play the silent game when I was on the other side.

After we crossed the border into Virginia, passing a sign that proclaimed, "Virginia is for Lovers," I finally caved and apologized. "I'm sorry for laughing," I said.

Grandpa Kalb didn't respond; he just kept staring out the window.

I continued, "I wasn't laughing at you. I just didn't expect someone your age to worry about something like that. That's all."

After a few more seconds of silence, Grandpa Kalb finally replied, "I'm not upset about the laughing. Sure, that bothered me a little, maybe even more than a little, but that's not what I'm thinking about."

"Then what is it?"

"It's what you said about your mother," Grandpa Kalb sighed. "Plus, the other stuff you've said about your mother. She wasn't always such a ... tight-ass."

"Ah," I said with a grin. "So, you admit that she is?"

"Sure. At times. And a lot of that is my fault."

Any satisfaction that I'd gotten from Grandpa Kalb acknowledging my mom's status as a tight-ass disappeared when I realized how much his role in that development pained him.

Grandpa Kalb continued, "I was always overprotective of

her. I had to be. She's the biggest blessing I ever got. She was our little miracle baby."

"What do you mean?"

"She was never supposed to be born. Back then, they didn't have all the fancy fertility treatments they do today, and even if they had, we probably wouldn't have been able to afford them. Nope, we had to rely on the old-fashioned way. We tried for over ten years to have a child, with no luck. Our doctor told us it wasn't gonna happen. It was hard on me, but it was even harder on your grandmother. She was so upset that she even stopped going to church for a while. Of course, three years after we gave up for good, along comes your mother."

"Wow," I said. "I had no idea about that." My mom had never talked about it, and I'd always just assumed my grandparents were a little older because they'd chosen to wait.

"Yeah, your mother still gets uncomfortable when I bring it up, so it doesn't surprise me that she hasn't." He took a deep breath and sighed. "All I've ever wanted is what was best for her. I just wanted her to have all the opportunities that we never had, and I busted my hump to give her everything I could. I pulled overtime so she could go to private school, and double-shifts so that she could be the first in the family to go to college."

"You never went to college?"

"I wish."

"That's crazy. They started talking to us about college in sixth grade. And I think my first career day was even earlier, like third grade."

Grandpa Kalb laughed, not a humorous laugh but more of a sarcastic one. "Yeah, well, that's another thing I never got to do," he said. "Back in the day, most people didn't get to choose their careers. Heck, I started working full time at the mill when I was

younger than you, and then I pretty much just had to keep
taking the best job I could get. I was lucky to eventually end up
working security at the Port Newark-Elizabeth Marine Terminal.
I actually didn't mind it. But that's why I pushed your mother,
maybe harder than I should have. I told her the truth early on,
that no one was gonna give her a damn thing and that she'd
have to outwork everyone else. And she did. Was it the right
way to raise a child? I don't know. We didn't have all the books
they do these days about that kind of stuff. But she's done some
great things. I think she could be the first female president if she
wanted to. And she seems happy ... some of the time." He went
back to staring out the window.

"Hey," I said, with enough enthusiasm that it startled my
grandpa, "you did the best you could, right?"

"Yeah," Grandpa Kalb said with a weak nod.

"Well, that's all anyone can ask for. Besides, she's actually
said the same exact stuff to me recently, so I'm pretty sure she
appreciates all the things you did for her. I mean, the lines would
probably work on me too, if I wasn't trying so hard to be a pain
in the ass."

Grandpa Kalb grinned. "Yeah, well, you do have a pretty
cushy life compared to your mother and being poor tends to
help. It's a pretty big motivator. I know it kept me busting my
butt."

"I bet," I said. I thought about all the things my grandpa had
experienced and how that had shaped the way he raised my
mom. I also thought about all the things I'd said about my mom,
none of which were flattering. "For the record, I do love my
mom. And my dad too. I just wish they'd stop fighting already.
It's like if they aren't gonna be together that's one thing, but why
do they have to keep fighting?"

"I don't know," Grandpa Kalb sighed. "They're both competitive people and don't like to lose. Whatever their reasons, it is sad. Your parents were a great couple."

"If they really were, they'd have stayed together like you and grandma."

"Not necessarily. I don't want you to think we were all roses. Your grandmother and I, we had our rough patches. This might be hard for you to believe, but I can be a stubborn asshole sometimes."

"Wait. You? No," I said with a grin.

Grandpa Kalb smiled back and said, "Hey! Don't smile too much. I think you inherited it from me."

"I think my mom and I both did."

"You're probably right." Grandpa Kalb paused for a second and then continued, "I think part of your parents' problem is that people as driven as them, require partners who are equally driven. But marriage isn't about personal achievements, and there comes a time in every relationship when each person needs to make sacrifices. When that time comes, ambitions can very easily get in the way."

"My parents' ambitions definitely got in the way. They're both at fault for that."

"Yeah, well, it was a lot easier when the gender roles were more rigid. There was no debate needed. Men worked and women focused on the home."

"I'm not gonna lie, that sounds pretty damn sexist."

"I didn't come up with it," Grandpa Kalb said defensively.

"I know," I said. "I'm just saying, for all your talk about the good old days, they don't really sound like they were that good. At least not for most people."

"Yeah, well, the truth is probably somewhere in the middle.

As a society, we've obviously taken steps forward in some ways, and in other ways, we've taken steps back. We aren't all better off just because we have computers, cell phones, and the Internet."

"How have we taken steps back?"

"For starters, people used to care a lot more about the elderly. They didn't just ship them off to homes; they took them into theirs. One of the biggest sacrifices I ever made was agreeing to let your grandmother's mother stay with us." He shook his head and exhaled deeply. "That woman had the most unpleasant disposition I'd ever seen, and for no reason. I used to joke that your grandmother must have sucked every ounce of happiness from her mother's body when she was in the womb. They were complete opposites. Your grandmother was always walking on sunshine. Her mother? That woman could shit on a rainbow."

I chuckled at my grandfather's description of my great-grandmother and the thought of him having to put up with her. "Maybe she's part of the reason people don't take their relatives in anymore," I said. "How many people did you tell about her?"

"Ha," Grandpa Kalb snickered. "Probably too many. You know what? That actually wouldn't surprise me. Leave it to her to ruin a good thing."

"What other sacrifices did you have to make for Grandma?"

"Remember how I told you she was afraid to fly? I was the opposite. I was a navigator in the service. I loved flying almost as much as I love baseball. But not even flying or baseball combined can make up a fraction of how much I loved your grandmother. Which is why we never flew anywhere. And now, I can't. There were other sacrifices, some big and some small, but at the end of the day, I have no regrets." He bit his lip and nodded a few times.

"This isn't a plane, but you're basically my navigator." I smiled at my grandpa.

"Yeah, I am," he said and smiled back. He turned serious, switching to what had to be his navigator's voice. "Let's get this bird to Baltimore. No colorful actions. Just keep it clean."

"Ten-four, Airman," I said and then slid my hands back up to ten and two and concentrated my focus on the road even tighter.

"Attaboy!" Grandpa Kalb exclaimed.

18

F our hours later, which would've been three and a half if not for the lunchtime traffic jam just outside of DC, we rounded a bend on the highway and downtown Baltimore came into view.

"Charm City," Grandpa Kalb proclaimed as the city's skyline grew in the windshield.

"How'd they get that nickname?" I asked.

"The only way you get a nickname like that."

"By having a lot of charm?"

"They wish," Grandpa Kalb chuckled. "No, they got it the same way they got their other nickname, The City That Reads, which they didn't get by reading a lot of books."

"How's that?"

"Just a bunch of advertisers getting into a room and spit-balling ideas." He smiled at me. "But I do like your optimistic take on it more."

"Me too."

"And Baltimore has given birth to a lot of great stuff. Actually, the Yankees started out in Baltimore for two years before moving to New York."

"No way."

"Yep. They were only here for two years. You know who else was born here besides your grandmother?"

"Easy," I said with a grin, "Grandma's cousin Eleanor."

"Actually, she was born in Essex, smartass."

"Fine. Edgar Allan Poe?" I'd heard Midnight rave about "The Raven" more than a few times and also complain about how the Baltimore football team was named after it, a "tragedy of epic proportions" in her mind. Although, to me, it seemed like a nice gesture.

"Wrong," Grandpa Kalb said, adding a fake buzzer noise for effect. "He was born in Boston. He did live in Baltimore for a while and died here too. You're only getting colder. Enough guessing. Just take the exit for downtown. I'll show you."

I took the exit for downtown Baltimore, and then we drove around for a minute until we found a parking spot. After feeding the meter with enough change to make sure we had all the time that we needed plus an additional half-hour—a move Grandpa Kalb insisted had kept him parking-ticket-free his whole life— we walked the couple blocks to Camden Yards, the home of the Baltimore Orioles baseball team.

"Isn't this enemy territory?" I asked as we approached the center field gate.

"Hardly," Grandpa Kalb said. "When the Yankees come to town, we take over the place. Plus, I wanted to show you this statue." He gestured to the sixteen-foot bronze statue just ahead. "It's part of your baseball education."

We were still far enough away that all I could do was make out the figure. It was a young, slim man in a baggy, old-time baseball uniform. He was holding a glove in one hand and resting the other on a baseball bat. When I got within ten feet, I was finally able to make out the writing on the plaque just below.

"George Herman 'Babe' Ruth," I read aloud. "That was Babe's real name?"

"You already know about Babe Ruth?" Grandpa Kalb said, half disappointed that I'd heard about him.

"Yeah, I don't know why. Maybe because of the candy bar."

"That's a Baby Ruth, and it's totally unrelated. Babe was arguably the greatest Yankee, if not player, to ever play the game. He was a once-in-a-lifetime hitter. And before that, he was actually a phenomenal pitcher."

"Why would the Orioles build a statue for him then?"

"Because the 'Bambino' was born just a couple of blocks from here. He actually signed his first contract with the Orioles, who were a minor league team at the time. You two have more in common than you know."

"How's that?"

"He was a little shit," Grandpa Kalb said with a grin. "He was born to two hard-working parents, another similarity, but he got in so much trouble that they had to send him to reform school. He was only half your age at the time."

"Damn," I said and shook my head. "They gave up on him early."

"So did the Red Sox. They traded him to the Yankees. That's how they got the curse." Grandpa Kalb gestured to the statue. "Anything about his name sound familiar to you?"

I read the plaque again. It was kind of familiar, but I couldn't place it. "Not really."

"Here's a hint," Grandpa Kalb said. "You ever hear me call

anyone my Bambino?"

I thought about it for a second and then remembered hearing it a couple of times, years earlier. "Yeah, you called my mom that."

"Bingo. If your mother would've been a boy, she would've been George Herman Kalb."

"But instead, you named her Georgia Helen Kalb."

"Exactly. It was the closest I could get your grandmother to sign off on."

"Why didn't you name her after Yogi?"

"Like I said, your grandmother had to sign off. There's no real way to make Yogi a girl's name. So, Georgia was our compromise."

I read over the plaque once more. The birth year and year of death were closer than I had expected. I did the quick math to determine his age of death. "Wow," I said, "he was only fifty-three when he died? What happened?"

Grandpa Kalb bit his lip and shook his head. "Brain tumor. I'll never forget when I heard the news that he passed. It was the summer after I turned eighteen. He fought the cancer for two years, just like your grandmother. He was actually one of the first people to get chemotherapy and radiation at the same time. They say that toward the end, he was in so much pain in his jaw that he couldn't even chew the white of an egg. He lost damn near 130 pounds."

"Jesus," I said. "That sounds terrible."

"It is terrible. It's always terrible. And the saying, 'The bigger they are, the harder they fall,' couldn't be truer for all the Yankee greats. DiMaggio died of lung cancer. Mickey Mantle got liver cancer, and that was after his son and mother died in the eighteen months before. But the craziest part is, they all might have had it easy compared to The Iron Horse."

"Lou Gehrig, right?" I said, remembering how he'd wanted my parents to name me after him. Grandpa Kalb solemnly nodded his head. The name also brought up another memory, but one I couldn't place. "Why do I feel like I've heard his name somewhere else?"

"You probably heard about him because of the disease they named after him."

"Yeah. That's it. I'm assuming he had that?"

"Yep," Grandpa Kalb said, nodding. "They didn't call it Lou Gehrig's disease at the time. That's what most people remember him for now. He should be remembered for the way he lived and not the way he died. He was my favorite player growing up and the best first baseman of all time. He had the record for most consecutive games played, held it for fifty-six years until Cal Ripken broke it about thirteen years ago at this very stadium. Lou probably would still have it if he hadn't gotten sick." Grandpa Kalb paused and swallowed hard. "It took one of the worst damn diseases in the world to take him out of the lineup. Your body goes while your mind stays intact. It's almost like what Walter's dealing with. And with all that, Lou still said he was the luckiest man in the world. He died two years and a month after his last game."

"What about Yogi?" I said, a little afraid to ask and hear the bad news.

"He's still going, thank the lord," Grandpa Kalb said. "I have a feeling he'll break the curse and pass in his sleep from natural causes. He was always lucky that way. He could make the best of any situation and almost never got punched out. I always said that he could turn shit into hits." Grandpa Kalb grinned. "Get it?"

"Yeah, I got that," I said, chuckling at the clever wordplay.

Grandpa Kalb sighed. "Most people aren't that lucky." He gently nodded his head for a few seconds and then said, "All right. It's time to go see your grandmother."

We headed back to the car, which still had forty minutes left on the meter, and then drove through downtown and a couple of small neighborhoods of varying degrees of niceness and not niceness. Along the way, Grandpa Kalb spotted a corner store and had me pull over. He ran inside and grabbed a dozen pink tulips and a couple of packages of Bergers cookies—which he claimed were the best cookies ever—and then we continued to a cemetery just outside of the city.

It had been almost exactly three years since I'd been to the cemetery, and my memory of where my grandma was buried was foggy at best. The one thing I did remember from the funeral was how overcome with emotion my mom had been. It was the first time I'd ever seen her like that. I don't think I'd ever seen her cry until that moment. She was unable to stop her tears from falling, and I was unable to do anything to help her.

Grandpa Kalb's memory was much better than mine. In the sea of seemingly identical granite slabs, he knew exactly where to go. He didn't even make one wrong turn. He carefully navigated the rows until we ended up at my grandma's grave. Chiseled in the headstone: Evelyn Marie Kalb; Born May 20th, 1932; Died September 15th, 2005.

Grandpa Kalb laid the flowers against the gravestone and then returned to my side. "It's time to say a prayer for your grandmother," he said.

I nodded in agreement. However, with my minimal religious upbringing, I wasn't quite sure what to do next. I let Grandpa Kalb lead the way and just followed his moves. He slowly went to his knees and then tapped his fingers on his forehead, belly, and then both shoulders, first left then right. He held his palms together at his chest and closed his eyes, and so did I. From there, I was on my own.

While I'd never formally prayed before, I'd had the occasional chat with God. Most of my little talks were mostly limited to me begging for things that I wanted for myself, like a special Christmas present, a birthday present, and other similar present-related requests. That time though, I asked God to take care of my grandma. I also asked God to watch over my grandpa and to help my parents find peace, whatever that meant.

As I wrapped up my prayer with an awkward goodbye to God, I noticed that all the lingering anger I'd held toward my parents was gone. It was replaced with a yearning to be with them and to apologize for the pain that I'd caused them. As much as I said that they wouldn't care that I was gone, I knew they were super worried and probably going crazy. I also knew that I wasn't going to run away anymore. I was going home.

I wanted to let them know that we were safe and that we would be coming back soon. Of course, I knew that I couldn't make the call just then. I couldn't do anything that would jeopardize making it to the game. I knew how much it meant to my grandpa, and I was determined to get us there no matter what, even if it meant stressing out my parents for a few more days.

While I couldn't call my parents, I knew exactly what I wanted to say to them when it was time. I was not only going to tell them how sorry I was for everything that I'd done, but I was also going to tell them how much I loved them. It had been way too long since I had told them that. I also knew that I needed to extend a similar apology to Derek and his parents, who had only done their best to try to help me.

After finishing my prayer, I opened my eyes and waited for my grandpa to open his.

A few seconds later, he did and said, "Amen."

"Amen," I said and then followed his lead with the finger tapping again before standing back up.

We stood there in silence for a moment and then Grandpa Kalb said, "Can I actually have a minute alone?"

"Sure," I said. "I can just go wait in the car."

"That would be great."

I took my time walking back to the Buick, checking on my grandpa every dozen or so steps to make sure he was okay. After I made it to the car, I climbed inside and waited.

A few minutes later, Grandpa Kalb joined me. His face was flushed, and his eyes were bloodshot. "Thanks for that," he said and then buckled his seatbelt.

"Of course," I said. I went to start the car and then stopped. "I have a question."

"What's that?"

"I noticed there was an empty space next to grandma's grave." I hadn't noticed it at the funeral, maybe because that was where we all had stood. "What's that for?"

"That's my plot," Grandpa Kalb said. "We purchased them almost fifty years ago. It wasn't my first choice. But your grandmother really wanted to be buried with her family, and I never wanted to leave her side." He sniffled, rubbed his nose, and then swallowed hard. "You know, Yogi had a great line about funerals."

"Why am I not surprised?" I said, grinning expectantly.

"He said, 'Always go to other people's funerals, otherwise they won't come to yours.'"

I made a show of laughing. In part because the line deserved it, but also because I was hoping that my amusement might help lift my grandpa's spirits.

Grandpa Kalb chuckled, but only for a brief moment. As soon as his snickering ceased, his eyes began welling up. I put my hand on his shoulder and smiled. Grandpa Kalb bit his lip and nodded, attempting to fight back his tears but losing the battle. "You wanna hear a funny story about your grandmother?" he asked.

"Of course," I said, my eyes welling up too.

"So, your grandmother grew up just a few miles from here, in a mostly German neighborhood called Highlandtown. But because of the funny Baltimore accents that everyone has here, they all called it 'Hollantown.' It wasn't until your grandmother was in her teens, and they put up a sign for the neighborhood, that she realized she'd been spelling it the wrong way. She even asked her dad what the heck Highlandtown was." Grandpa Kalb giggled and then wiped away the tears that had broken free.

"That is hilarious," I said and did the same.

"Yeah. It is. But don't go thinking that your grandmother was dumb."

"I never have and never would."

"Good. Because she was as sharp as a tack. She could solve any crossword puzzle and always knew every answer on *Jeopardy*. Most of the smarts your mother got, she got from her. Most of my brain space is filled up with nothing but baseball stats."

"Speaking of that," I said, "any idea who's on the mound tonight?"

"Are you kidding me? I know the starters for the next two

weeks. Tonight, the Orioles got Burress, and we got Aceves. It should be another close one. And the close ones are …" He looked to me for the answer.

"The best ones," I said.

19

A few hours plus eight and a half innings later, the game was in the bottom of the ninth, and the Yankees and Orioles were all knotted up at zero. Grandpa Kalb and I sat on the edge of our king-sized hotel bed with our shirts flipped inside out and our nails practically chewed off. We'd switched to our "rally shirts" with one out in the fourth inning, which was the only time the Yankees had gotten more than one runner on base during the whole game.

Grandpa Kalb had insisted that we "live it up" on our last night before the big game, and so we booked the best room at the best hotel in Baltimore. Unfortunately, that room happened to be the InterContinental Harbor Court's penthouse couple's suite, which meant that we would be sharing a bed. However, it also meant marble tile, silk linens, and floor-to-ceiling windows with spectacular views of the Inner Harbor. Of course, neither of us paid much attention to the view because we were too engrossed in the deadlocked game.

"This is too close," I said, my nervous energy getting the better of me. "It's gone from good to bad."

"As long as we win, it's still good," Grandpa Kalb said. "Although, I think we might've jinxed the team by staying in Baltimore. I should've known this would happen. It's happened a lot before, almost every time we'd come to visit."

"I think we need to switch our shirts back. I think we jumped the gun on the rally shirts."

"I think you're right. It wasn't really rally worthy. It's a good thing we still have time."

"It ain't over until it's over," I said and winked at my grandpa.

"Exactly. But we need to hurry up because Jeter's stepping up to the plate."

We furiously worked to remove our shirts, which only made the act that much more challenging. By the time we'd gotten our shirts off, Jeter had already seen three pitches, two balls and one strike, and the next one was on the way. The pitch drilled Jeter on the hand.

"That bastard!" I said. "He hit Jeter."

"We'll take it," Grandpa Kalb said. "We need the runners. They'll probably pinch-run Gardner since he's got better speed. This is all good."

"I hope so." I reversed my shirt to the right side out and was about to put my arm through the sleeve when Grandpa Kalb stopped me, firmly grabbing my hand.

"Hold your horses. We got the runner with our shirts off. The first runner in a while. We need to see where this goes. We need to let it play out."

Grandpa Kalb was right about two things, our shirts had been off for the hit by pitch and the Yankees did end up pinch-running Brett Gardner. On the first pitch to Bobby Abreu, which was a ball, Gardner took off for second base, and Grandpa Kalb and I jumped out of our seats.

"He's stealing!" I shouted.

"Safe!" Grandpa Kalb screamed, mimicking the umpire's safe gesture.

"It's working. He's in scoring position!"

"Damn straight! It's a shirtless rally! No more shirts the rest of the way!"

Three straight balls later, the last of which was intentional, Bobby Abreu jogged to first base, and our shirtless rally was looking promising.

"Time to end it, A-Rod," Grandpa Kalb shouted, swinging his shirt in a circle like a lasso as Alex Rodriguez stepped into the batter's box.

Unfortunately, A-Rod didn't end anything except his at-bat. With an 0-2 count, he hit a weak roller to second base. If there was one positive, it was that the roller was so soft that the Orioles couldn't turn a double play. A-Rod got the fielder's choice and Gardner was able to make it to third.

"All we need is a sac fly," I said, swinging my shirt like my grandpa.

"Giambi is just the man for the job," he said.

Jason Giambi worked the count full, but on the final pitch, he swung over the top of the ball and struck out.

"No!" I shouted and buried my head in between my knees. As I sat with my thighs clamping my head, the ridiculousness of the whole situation crossed my mind. I mean, just two days earlier, I couldn't have cared less about the Yankees. But now, I was reacting—or overreacting—like I had something at stake in the game; because, as unlikely as it would have seemed before, I did. I yanked my head up and turned to my grandpa. "The shirtless rally is dead. We need something else. Should we take off our pants?"

"Not yet. We still have one out left," Grandpa Kalb said. "And besides, A-Rod stole second, which means they will walk Nady so there's a play at every base. Which also means, your boy Cano is gonna get to come through."

Like usual, at least when pertaining to baseball, Grandpa Kalb was right. I had missed A-Rod's stolen base while my head was in between my legs. With first base open, the Orioles walked Nady, leaving it all up to Cano.

As Robinson stepped into the batter's box, my old friends, the pterodactyls, started thrashing in my stomach. It was possibly the most active they'd ever been. The only time that really came close was the first time I'd kissed Grace. However, realistically, I was less nervous about that. Partly, because it came out of nowhere, so there was no time for anticipation, but also because I didn't kiss her as much as she kissed me.

We'd been watching *Sixteen Candles* at my house after school, and the movie was just about over. It was on the final scene, where Molly Ringwald and Matt Dillon kiss over a lit birthday cake, because teens in the '80s weren't as aware of obvious fire hazards. Grace turned to me and asked, "Do you want to kiss me?" The question had barely registered in my brain, the pterodactyls only getting in a few violent flaps, before she leaned in and kissed me. I spent the first half of the kiss mentally pinching myself and the other half realizing that I should put more effort into making sure I was doing a good job. It was soft, sweet, and over before I knew it.

If the build-up to the kiss had been anything like the bottom of the ninth inning, I probably wouldn't have survived. As it was, I was barely surviving the inning. My body was shaking like Yankee Stadium before the last out of game six in 1977, all my nervous energy waiting to charge the field.

"I don't know how long I'll be able to take this," I said. I was fairly certain that if the at-bat went to a full count, my heart and stomach would most likely explode.

"Just breathe," Grandpa Kalb said. "And let Robbie make them pay."

I took a deep breath but forgot to exhale as the first pitch came down the pike. Thankfully, Cano wasted no time, swinging at the pitch, and lacing a single to center field. All the air exploded from my lungs, and Grandpa Kalb and I leaped out of our seats.

"That's how you make them pay!" Grandpa Kalb shouted.

"And that's why he's my favorite player!" I added.

Grandpa Kalb and I hugged each other and traded enthusiastic back slaps.

"That was awesome!" I said, still trying to catch my breath.

"You bet your ass it was. And on top of that, it looks like the Red Sox are losing. This is a cause for celebration." He thought about it for a split second, and then his face perked up. "And I have just the idea," he said as he wiggled his eyebrows.

Grandpa Kalb grabbed a couple of the bottle rockets he'd bought from South of the Border and one of the empty cans of Mountain Dew that was sitting on the coffee table. He shoved the fireworks' stabilizing sticks into the Mountain Dew opening and twisted their fuses together. "Since I only have so many hands, I'm gonna need your help with the matches."

"Are you sure this is a good idea?" I asked.

"No. In fact, I'm pretty sure it isn't," he said with a grin. "Just don't tell your mother about this or try this at home." He opened the window as much as he could, which was only halfway, and stuck his arm and the can and fireworks outside.

I retrieved the small box of matches that had come with the fireworks and had a cartoon drawing of Pedro the bandito on the cover. I took a match, struck it against the side, and then extended the tiny fire out the window, cupping it with my hand to protect it from the wind. I held it up to the wrapped fuses, which caught immediately and kicked back sparks. The sparks increased as the flames reached the tiny tubes of gunpowder. Grandpa Kalb and I screamed with excitement as the bottle rockets took flight, leaving faint streaks of smoke and flames in the night's sky before exploding with weak pops over the harbor.

We yanked our arms back inside and fell to the floor. We were giggling like a couple of little kids at a sleepover watching late-night Cinemax for the first time when someone shouted from the street below, "Hey! You can't do that!"

"What are you, a cop?" Grandpa Kalb shouted back. He turned to me and shook his head. "That jackass thinks he's the law."

Grandpa Kalb was still shaking his head when the stranger yelled back, "Yeah! I am a cop."

Grandpa Kalb's eyes went wide.

"You think he's for real?" I said.

"I don't know. But if he's just messing with us"—Grandpa Kalb brandished a bottle rocket—"I'm firing one of these puppies right at his keister."

"I really hope he isn't a cop."

"Me too."

We both slowly peeked out the window. Sure enough, standing five stories below was a uniformed police officer. "I see you up there," he shouted and pointed at us. "I'll be up in a second to give both of you tickets."

"He can't come up here," I whispered through gritted teeth. "He'll bust us. We'll have to go home. What do we do?"

"The only thing we can do," Grandpa Kalb responded under his breath. "We kiss the hell out of his butt." He shouted down to the officer, "I'm so sorry, Officer. We just got a little excited. We know how tough your job is, and the last thing I would ever want to do is distract you from keeping the people of this great city safe."

"It won't happen again," I added. "We promise."

"Swear on my life. You won't even hear a peep from us."

The officer just stood there, staring up at us, still undecided.

"It didn't work," I whispered. "What do we do now?"

"You know what to do," Grandpa Kalb whispered back.

I knew exactly what he was talking about. Like two synchronized swimmers going for the gold, we both smiled, raised our hands in unison, and waved. We kept waving for a few seconds, before the officer finally waved back and then headed on his way.

Grandpa Kalb slammed the window closed, and I yanked the curtains shut.

"It worked!" I shouted as I jumped up and down. "I can't believe your move worked!"

"What are you talking about?" Grandpa Kalb said, jumping with me. "Of course it did. It always—" His feet hit the ground with a thud, and his face contorted as he and doubled over. "Ah," he moaned and pressed his palms against his eye sockets.

"Are you okay?" I asked and put my hand on his back. "Is everything all right?"

Grandpa Kalb let a few more groans before lifting his head

back up. "It's fine," he said, still wincing. "It's just a glaucoma flare-up."

"Is there anything I can do to help?"

"No. I just have to ride it out." He held his breath as he fought off another burst of pain and then exhaled. "It should go away after a while. Like an hour or two."

"You don't have anything you can take?"

"No. Nothing."

"How could there not be—" I stopped short as we both had the same realization. There was something he could take: the Marinol.

"No," Grandpa Kalb said. "I'm not taking that. I could go crazy."

"If that was really a possibility, do you think your doctor would've given it to you?"

My grandpa was considering the truth I'd dropped on him when he got hit by another short attack.

After it passed, I added, "You know I'm right. Besides, everyone I know that's tried it says it just makes them relaxed and want to eat junk food. That's pretty much what you've been doing anyway."

My grandpa considered what I'd said. After about fifteen seconds, his face relaxed. "Fine," he said, "but I'm not doing it by myself."

"Why not?" I said. The proposition of trying marijuana, in any form, with my grandpa, for both of our first times, was too incredibly ridiculous of an opportunity to pass up.

Grandpa Kalb and I each popped one of the dark, spherical pills that looked like gel BBs, chased them with swigs of Mountain Dew, and then waited for the magic to kick in.

THIRTY MINUTES after ingesting our tiny THC pills, we were still waiting for even the slightest tingle and getting more and more anxious by the second.

"I still don't feel anything," I said as I paced the room.

"Me either," Grandpa Kalb agreed as he crossed my path, pacing in the opposite direction.

"How old are they?"

"I've had them for about a year."

"Maybe they're expired." I grabbed the pill bottle from the table and read the expiration. "It says they're still good for another six months."

"They don't go bad when they expire anyway," Grandpa Kalb said. "They just get weaker."

"Oh. Well, maybe they got weaker early like Yogi said," I said as our pacing crossed paths again.

"Maybe. You really need to stop pacing. You're making me nervous."

"I was only pacing because you started pacing."

"I started the pacing?"

I nodded.

"I need to sit down," Grandpa Kalb said. "I need some kind of distraction."

I grabbed the TV remote and tossed it to my grandpa. He turned on the TV and flipped through the channels. "Perfect," he said as he found some Western movie on the free HBO. "If you haven't seen *Blazing Saddles*, you haven't lived. The movie is hilarious, and Mel Brooks is a goddamn genius!"

I'd never heard of Mel Brooks, nor seen *Blazing Saddles*. But after watching the movie for ten minutes, I agreed with my grandpa. The movie was ridiculous and probably offensive to a lot of people, but it was also unbelievably funny. Grandpa Kalb and I took turns suffering from severe laugh attacks. And then, a few minutes into our relay of hysterics, just when it was my turn to take over, Grandpa Kalb started wheezing uncontrollably, like he was choking.

"Are you okay?" I said.

He shook his head, no, and rolled over.

"What's wrong?" I hurried to flip him back over and see what was wrong.

Grandpa Kalb's face was squinched and growing a deeper shade of red with each millisecond, and then he exploded like a balloon, spitting air and laughter. "I am stoned out of my freaking mind!"

I let out a deep sigh. "You scared me!" I said and then went stiff. At that very moment, I realized that I couldn't feel my toes. The numb, tingling sensation quickly moved through my feet and up my legs to my stomach, chest, and head, and then out to my arms, spreading through my body like warm Velveeta cheese until I was completely covered like a human nacho.

"Me too," I said in the most serious voice I could muster. "I don't feel anything ... in my body!" I burst into another spastic fit.

"Me either," Grandpa Kalb said in between struggling breaths.

It took us over a minute to regain our composure. When we finally did, Grandpa Kalb added, "Why was I so afraid of this stuff."

"I don't know," I said. "Why was I?"

"You're young. It's good to have a little fear. It keeps you safe. Just don't go making a habit out of stuff like this."

"I won't," I said. "I'll save it for special occasions, like Yankees victories."

"Perfect," Grandpa Kalb said with a giggle, and then stopped suddenly. "Wait a second! That's way too many occasions."

"I'm kidding," I said. "It was a joke."

We both had a long laugh.

"I don't know why people say that it leads to more drugs," Grandpa Kalb said. "The only thing I want to do is eat tons of food. I just wanna stuff my face with everything."

"It's the munchies," I said. "I totally have them too. Where's your stash?"

"I'll get it!" Grandpa Kalb crawled out of bed. I wasn't sure if he was moving really slow, or if time had just slowed down, or if it was some combination of the two, but he moved at less than a snail's pace. He grabbed his grocery bag of goodies and started picking through it, tossing any trash he found in the air. By the time he reached the bottom of the bag, empty wrappers were all he'd found. "No!" he said. "We're out of snacks! How did we eat two packs of Bergers cookies already?"

"Easy," I said. "It was a long game, and they're so good."

"So good," Grandpa Kalb agreed, soothed by the memory of how delicious the cookies were. "I knew I should've grabbed another pack. Or at least some Tastykakes. What are we gonna do? We're screwed."

"It's okay," I said. "I'm sure they have a vending machine or two by the big icemaker. All hotels do."

"Good call. No, that's a great call! I'll tell you what. You're an ideas man. That's what you are. And everyone can always use an ideas man."

I accepted his compliment with a grin and then we both scurried out of the room in search of snacks.

"I want one of everything," I said as we practically floated down the hall.

"Screw that," Grandpa Kalb said. "I want two of everything."

"That means we need at least three of everything."

Unfortunately, we found nothing of anything. After scouring the whole floor, along with the one above and below, we didn't find a single ice maker or a vending machine.

"What kind of hotel is this?" I said as we headed back to our room, still incredibly high but slightly less happy.

"Too nice of a hotel if you ask me," Grandpa Kalb said. "We probably have to call for room service, but they might not even be open."

"If they are," I said, "I still want one of everything."

"Done."

We rounded a corner, where a middle-aged hotel guest waited for the elevator.

"Good evening, sir," Grandpa Kalb said politely.

"Yes, top of the evening to you, sir?" I added.

Not only did the man not respond, but he also did everything he could to avoid eye contact with us.

"What an asshole," I said when the man was out of earshot.

"Don't worry about him," Grandpa Kalb said. "Just keep your eyes on the prize."

After another turn down the hall, we were finally back at our room. We both stared at the door for a good five seconds before Grandpa Kalb said, "Well, aren't you gonna open the door?"

"I was waiting for you to open it," I said.

"How would I open it? You're the one with the key."

"No, I'm not. You are."

"I told you to get it," Grandpa Kalb said.

I thought about it for a second. That definitely never happened. "No, you didn't."

"Hmmm," Grandpa Kalb said, reconsidering. "Maybe I just thought that then."

"Yeah, I think so."

"Shit. Well, I guess we'll have to swing by the front desk."

"Maybe that's where the vending machines are," I said, trying to be optimistic.

"Fingers crossed."

We went back down the hall and took the elevator to the lobby. On our way down, the elevator opened for a middle-aged woman. She took one look at us and said that she'd take the next elevator. Then, when we got to the lobby, the night desk attendant, some balding man in his thirties, took one look at us and rolled his eyes as we approached.

"Did you see that?" I whispered under my breath to my grandpa. "Everyone here is so stuck up."

"Don't worry," Grandpa Kalb whispered. "Let me handle this." He gave a friendly nod to the night desk attendant and smiled as we approached the front desk. "Good evening, sir. We have a bit of a problem."

"You don't say," the night desk attendant said, stifling laughter.

"I do. I don't want to bore you with the details, but we've been locked out of our room."

"I can't imagine how that happened." The night desk attendant couldn't help but let out a little of his laughter. "I'm sorry," he said, but instead of stopping, he just giggled even more.

"Hey!" Grandpa Kalb said, with a look of death in his eyes. "I'll have you know, this isn't my first time staying at a nice hotel. I've stayed at much nicer places—at least two. And I didn't bust my ass for sixty years and serve this country in Korea to be treated like some second-class citizen by you and other guests of this goddamn place."

The night desk attendant covered his mouth with his fist and extinguished any remaining amusement he had left. "I am truly sorry about that, sir," he said, his voice finally matching his words.

"And you should be."

"I appreciate your service and did not mean to be disrespectful. It's just that—"

"It's just that what?" Grandpa Kalb glared at the night desk attendant, ready to rip him a new one.

The night desk attendant swallowed hard and said, "It's just that it's hard to take you seriously when neither of you are wearing shirts."

Grandpa Kalb and I turned to each other. I looked him up and down, and he did the same. We were so stoned and caught up in our search for food that, until the attendant mentioned it, we both had completely overlooked the fact that our shirts were still off. Realistically, they had every reason to be looking at as funny, because we looked ridiculous. We both chuckled.

"That is ... definitely a valid point," Grandpa Kalb said, trying to sound as professional as possible while fighting back his laughter. "I can see where you're coming from on that."

"It was a shirtless rally," I added, and then covered my mouth and looked away.

"I see," the night desk attendant said and handed Grandpa Kalb our new keys.

"Thanks. You don't have any vending machines, do you?"

"No."

"What about room service?" Grandpa Kalb said. "How late do they run?"

"24 hours."

"Perfect. Well, we really appreciate your help. We'll get out of your hair and go put shirts on."

"Enjoy your stay."

We nodded, said thanks, and then calmly made our way back to the elevator. After we'd stepped inside and the doors had closed, I said, "You do realize you just told a balding guy that we'd get out of his hair, right?"

Grandpa Kalb just nodded, his whole face clenched as he fought to contain the energy building inside him. His head began to twitch, then shake, before finally exploding. We both fell to the ground, our bodies convulsing on the tile floor. I'd never laughed so hard or for so long in my entire life.

20

I n our Marinol-induced stupor, Grandpa Kalb and I had not only neglected to put our shirts back on, but we had also neglected to close the blackout blinds. The next morning, I woke up with the hot sun beating down on my face. I rolled over to find Grandpa Kalb still passed out beside me, his head buried under the pillow.

I crawled out of bed, every muscle in my body sore from all of our laughing. Even muscles I didn't know I had were sore. My abs were in the worst shape though. They felt like I'd done a thousand crunches. After some ineffective stretching, I navigated the traffic jam of room service carts parked throughout the suite as I made my way to the bathroom and then hopped in the shower. I turned the handle to extra hot and let the near-boiling beads of water bring life back to my aching body.

Just like the morning before, my thoughts quickly drifted to Grace. I couldn't wait to get back home and tell her all about the trip and my night on Marinol with my grandpa. I couldn't wait to finally share happy stories with her. No more complaining about my parents and loading all of my burdens on her—never again. From that point forward, I swore that I would only build her up and never bring her down. Of course, that would only come after I'd won her back. But I knew that I would win her back, everything else was just a formality. And after I had, I knew she'd die laughing hearing about the adventures that my grandpa and I'd had. However, our biggest adventure was still to come. It was game day, we were just a little over two-hundred miles from Yankee Stadium, and I couldn't wait to experience the last game with my grandpa.

After finishing my shower, drying off, and getting dressed, I returned to the room to find Grandpa Kalb still snoozing with no sign of waking up. I cleared my throat, making as much noise as I could, but it didn't stir him at all. Given how late our night had gone and knowing that we had just a few hours left to drive, I decided to let him keep sleeping. I also figured there was a good chance he'd probably just snore himself awake in the next few minutes anyway.

While I waited, I grabbed the newspaper—the morning's copy of the *Baltimore Sun*, which had been left outside of our room—and sat down on the couch to peruse the pages. I was surprised to find that most of the front of the sports section was taken up by an article about the end of Yankee Stadium. In the article, there were a lot of interesting facts that Grandpa Kalb had yet to mention.

Apparently, Knute Rockne had given his famous "Win one for the Gipper" speech there, and they even had a boxing match at the stadium, where Joe Louis knocked out some German guy in the first round. The fight had taken place around the same time that the Nazis were taking over Germany, and many people said it was one of the most important sporting events of the 20th century. Another tidbit that I really liked was that they were planning to preserve the field and use it as a Little League diamond.

After I finished the article, I skimmed over a couple more stories in the sports section and then checked the clock. It was a little before nine, and I knew Grandpa Kalb would want to be on the road soon, if not already. I got up and walked to the bed. I grabbed Grandpa Kalb's shoulder and shook it gently. His skin was warm to the touch, and my shake did nothing to rouse him. I tried again, this time harder. Still nothing. I started to get seriously worried. I started to think something had happened to him. I didn't want to think about what. I grabbed both of his shoulders and prepared to shake him as hard as I could.

Before I got the chance, Grandpa Kalb let out a cough and a full body shiver. I let go of his shoulders and got off the bed, not wanting to freak him out.

After a mixture of mumbles and groans, Grandpa Kalb finally opened his eyes and grinned. "Wow. You look ready to go. I can't believe you woke up before me again."

"Yeah, I beat you by over an hour," I said. "Me and the early bird were having a chat about you over a couple of worms."

"I hope it was only good things." He chuckled at his own joke and then winced.

"Are you okay?"

"Yeah. All this traveling is finally catching up to me. And my muscles are pretty sore from last night and all that laughing."

"Mine too. I haven't laughed that hard or for that long ever."

"Me either. It was a great time."

"Yeah. We'll have to do that again."

Grandpa Kalb massaged his temples for a moment before responding, "We sure will."

"Well, I'm ready to go whenever you are," I said.

"Just give me a few minutes, and I'll be good to go." Grandpa Kalb struggled to sit up. As much as my body was beat from the night before, it looked like he had it much worse.

I grabbed his arm with one hand and supported his back with the other to help him.

"Thanks," Grandpa Kalb said and hunched over on the edge of the bed.

"I'll get your medicine," I said and started to weave through the carts toward his suitcase.

"That's okay," he said, holding up his hand. "I don't need them today."

I stopped. "Why not?"

"Because, uh ... you know? It's Sunday. It's a day of rest. Haven't you ever heard that?"

"Yeah. But I thought that was just a religious thing, not a medical thing."

"Well, my doctor must be religious too, because for the stuff they have me on that's how they do it. It's various regimes for six days of the week and then nothing on Sunday. It's like a detox."

It sounded kind of strange, but my experience with medication had been limited to over-the-counter ibuprofen for headaches and the occasional round of antibiotics for my yearly sinus infections. I looked at my grandpa, who shot me a toothy grin. "Cool," I said, smiling back.

"Yep," he said. "Modern medicine. It's all very cool."

THIRTY MINUTES LATER, we were back on the highway. It would've been less time, but before we'd left the hotel, Grandpa Kalb made a point of switching into what he dubbed his game day gear: a number 8 jersey and a satin Yankees jacket. The Y on the back of the jacket had been colored hot pink, which my grandpa explained was from when my mom was four years old and had decided to "make it pretty" with her brand-new set of markers.

As we drove, Grandpa Kalb rehashed the top ten games that he'd attended at Yankee Stadium. He was on number eight when he went suddenly silent.

I checked on him out of the corner of my eye. I watched Grandpa Kalb shift in his seat, trying to get comfortable, and then he raised the back of his hand to his forehead, gauging his temperature. "Everything all right over there?" I asked.

"Of course," Grandpa Kalb said. "I'm just running a little hot. That's par for the course on Sundays, on account of all the toxins leaving the body."

"Oh."

"Speaking of toxins leaving the body, I need to hit the latrine if you wanna get off at the next exit. It's also probably a good idea to gas up before we hit the turnpike. They really gouge you on gas there."

"Sure," I said, somewhat surprised he needed to make a bathroom stop this early or even at all. "What happened to your adult diapers?"

"I miscalculated how much whizzing I'd be doing. I already went through my whole stash."

"Do you want to pick some more up?"

"That's okay. They only come in big packs, and I hate having extras."

I took the next exit toward Bel Air/Edgewood and pulled into the Wawa gas station just off of the freeway. Grandpa Kalb lumbered inside to hit the bathroom, grab some more drinks—since he was "dying of thirst"—and pay for the gas while I manned the pump.

The tank was three-quarters full, so it didn't take long to fill up. After finishing at the pump, I moved the car to a parking space in front and waited for my grandpa. A couple minutes later, he exited with two six packs of Mountain Dew in tow.

"Buy one get one free," Grandpa Kalb explained as he climbed back into the car. He cracked a can, slamming it before we made it back to the freeway. The caffeine seemed to have the opposite effect on him. "I think I'm still beat from last night," he explained as he yawned. "You think you'll be all right if I get some more shut eye?"

"I think so," I said. "Are there any special instructions or directions I need to know?"

"Nope. Just stay on 95. You'll hit a bridge toll pretty soon and the turnpike not long after that." He retrieved a couple twenties from his wallet and handed them to me. "In case I'm not up by then. You can keep the change."

"Thanks."

Grandpa Kalb smiled, closed his eyes, and was out faster than a batter facing Mariano Rivera.

I drove for the next hour with just my thoughts and the soft radio playing in the background; however, I didn't hear a single song. I was busy thinking about my grandpa, something didn't seem right. He didn't seem right.

Every few minutes, I would glance over to make sure he was doing okay. And every couple of minutes, his cheeks changed like Home Depot paint swatches showcasing a deeper shade of red as his breaths grew heavier.

We were just outside of the New Jersey suburbs of Philadelphia, and Grandpa Kalb's cheeks were approaching what Sherwin-Williams refers to as "Heartthrob" red, when I decided to reach over and check my grandpa's forehead for myself. My hand was only a couple inches away, and I could already feel the heat radiating from his forehead, when his dry gums smacked and his face puckered. I yanked my hand back just before Grandpa Kalb opened his eyes, returning it to the steering wheel, ten and slightly more than two.

Grandpa Kalb stretched, yawned, and then squinted at me. I must have been doing a terrible job hiding the fact that I'd almost been busted, because his first words were, "What are you up to over there? You look like you're up to something."

"Nothing," I said, keeping my eyes on the road. "Just driving. That's about it."

Grandpa Kalb waited a moment before responding. "If you say so. You might want to slide that right hand up a little. It's getting close to two-thirty, which is a dentist's favorite time." He chuckled at his own joke. "You get it? Two-thirty. Like tooth hurty."

"Oh, yeah," I said, feigning amusement.

Grandpa Kalb grabbed another can of Mountain Dew and put it down in two gulps. "Next rest stop you see, pull over."

IT WAS another five miles before we hit the James Fenimore Cooper Service area, and I pulled off the turnpike. Named after the author who was known for writing "The Last of the Mohicans," the service area was the last of the rest stops that gave guests the chance to dine at either Burger King, Carvel, Cinnabon, or Popeye's without crossing the street.

I waited in the car, tapping my fingers on the steering wheel, while Grandpa Kalb went to the bathroom. A couple minutes passed, and I started to get worried again. Then five minutes passed, and my worry turned to what-ifs. A handful of people had entered the restroom after my grandpa, and each of them had already exited. At ten minutes, all the potential scenarios running through my mind were of the catastrophic nature, and I couldn't wait any longer. I hopped out of the car and sprinted toward the restroom.

I ripped open the door, half-expecting to find Grandpa Kalb lying on the restroom floor. Thankfully, he wasn't. He was upright and waiting on the other side of the entrance. His hair was soaking wet, and he had a perplexed look on his face.

"I thought you didn't need to go," he said and then passed by me as he exited the restroom.

"I didn't," I said. "You were just taking so long. I wanted to make sure everything was okay in there."

"Aside from the smell, which I had nothing to do with, everything was great."

"Why's your hair all wet?"

"I was just washing off. I've been getting so hot in the car." He started to walk back toward the car.

"Are you forgetting something?"

Grandpa Kalb shook his head. "I don't think so."

"What about your jacket?" I pointed to his jacket, which he'd left on the bathroom counter, most likely taking it off when he washed his hair.

"Oh, yeah, you mind grabbing that for me."

"Yeah. Sure," I said. I watched him lumber back toward the Buick for a few more feet before I slipped inside the rancid restroom and retrieved his jacket. He was right about the smell, but he was wrong about being all right. He could tell me he was fine, but I knew better. There was definitely something going on with him. I just didn't know exactly what it was, how bad it might be, or why he was lying to me.

21

Within ten minutes of being back on the turnpike, Grandpa Kalb had slammed another Mountain Dew and passed out again. While he slept, I struggled to come up with a way to get to the bottom of what was really going on. It was the only way that I could help him. I just didn't want to make him angry. It had been a while since he'd shown his temper, but I knew it was pretty easy to set him off. And, for all I knew, an exploding tantrum might make his condition worse. It would definitely get his heart rate up, which could maybe give him a heart attack or something.

Unfortunately, after forty-five minutes of thinking outside of the box, inside of the box, and everywhere in between the box, I still hadn't come up with a plan. The only thing I'd determined was that, whatever was going on, he seemed to be in complete denial about it. As the Manhattan skyline came into view, taking up the entire windshield and part of the passenger-side window, my plotting was forced to take a backseat. I gave Grandpa Kalb a gentle nudge.

"Hey," he mumbled as he slowly came to. "What the hell's going on?"

I wanted to say that I was wondering the same thing. Instead, I just said, "We're getting close. I need directions."

Grandpa Kalb glanced out the window, checking the signs and gathering his bearings. "Yeah. Of course," he said. "Just ... uh ... let me think for a second." A few seconds later, he continued, "Just stay on 95 until we cross the George Washington Bridge. Then take the Major Deegan Expressway toward Queens. There should be signs after that."

"Thanks," I said. I drove silently for a moment, hoping the right words to get the real conversation started would come to me, but they never did. Right words or not, I knew I had to say something. So, I just got straight to the point as gently as possible. "I think something might be wrong," I said.

"What are you talking about?" Grandpa Kalb said, surprised. "With the car? Is it making a noise? It should be fine. Walt had it tuned up last week."

"No," I said and took a deep breath. "With you. I really think something's wrong with you."

Grandpa Kalb closed his eyes, shook his head a few times, and then reopened his lids. "I appreciate the concern, but I'm fine."

I waited a moment before responding, "You don't seem fine."

"Well, I am," he said firmly.

"I think we should maybe stop by an urgent care really quick," I countered, keeping my tone soft, "just to make sure that everything is all right. It can't hurt."

Grandpa Kalb exhaled harshly and shook his head a few more times. I could see his frustration building with each shake. "The only thing that's not 'all right' with me, is the fact that you keep asking me if I'm all right, and I keep telling you I am, but you refuse to believe me, goddamnit!"

"I'm sorry," I said. "I'm not trying to make you mad. All I'm saying is that you seem different today."

"I'm different today?" He chuckled, not a cheerful one, more indignant amusement. "Compared to what? Compared to the other three days over the past year that you've seen me. That's not even close to enough of a sample size for you to tell me what the hell I'm supposed to be like or whether I'm all right."

He was right about that. I hadn't been there. I hadn't seen him. But even with my limited exposure, I was still confident something was wrong.

Still fuming, Grandpa Kalb continued, "This is how every Saturday is. It's what I go through every Saturday. But you don't come by enough to know that. If I say I'm all right, then I'm goddamn all right."

There was something off about his response, but it took a moment for what was wrong to register. I turned and looked at him. "Grandpa, it's Sunday."

"I don't give a damn what day it is!" he said. "All I care about is that you keep your damn eyes on the damn road. This is big-city driving. A lot can happen in a short period of time. We're too close to the stadium to not get to the game."

I turned back to the road. I didn't need to say anything more. If there had been even a sliver of doubt inside me before our little clash, it had been removed, plucked by the tweezers of Grandpa Kalb's tirade. He wasn't on a detox—he'd chosen to stop taking his medicine.

GRANDPA KALB WAS RIGHT ABOUT big-city driving. It took all of my attention to safely maneuver the congested roads. Neither of us spoke a word the rest of the drive until Grandpa Kalb pointed and instructed me to make a right into the Days Inn parking lot.

After checking in, Grandpa Kalb gave me a key to the room, which he hadn't done at the previous hotels, and said, "Don't forget we're in 374. It's easy to remember because it's Ruth's, Mantle's, and Gehrig's jersey numbers. That means it's a lucky room." He smiled. When I didn't smile back, he added in a gentle tone, "Listen, I'm sorry about blowing up back in the car. I didn't mean what I said. It's just, I'm all right, okay?"

"Okay," I said with a weak smile.

"Good. Let's go to the room so I can hit the head, and then we'll figure out our next move."

We took the elevator to our third-floor room. Grandpa Kalb insisted on carrying his suitcase the entire way, refusing my offers to help. Once in the room, he tossed his bag on the bed and then made a beeline for the bathroom. Just before the door, he stopped and turned to me with a child-like grin on his face.

"I just remembered a great joke," he said. "Wanna hear it?"

I didn't respond. I was too busy thinking about my next move.

"I'll tell you anyway," Grandpa Kalb said. "A Yankee fan traveled to Boston to watch the Yankees crush the Red Sox at Fenway. During the game, he happens to go to the bathroom at the same time as a Red Sox fan. They both handle their business at the urinal. The Red Sox fan finishes, then starts to wash his hands. The Yankee fan finishes and then goes to leave." As the last word left Grandpa Kalb's tongue, his face went blank. It was as if all the wheels turning in his head had come to a sudden and grinding halt, and the only thing he remembered was that he'd been speaking. "Uh, what was I saying?"

"You were telling me the joke about the Yankee fan and the Red Sox fan," I said.

The wheels started back up, albeit slowly. "Oh, yeah," Grandpa Kalb said, gradually gaining more memory steam. "Of course. How could I forget? So, the Yankee fan finishes and then goes to leave. And the Red Sox fan says, 'Excuse me, but in Boston, we're taught to wash our hands after we go to the bathroom.' And the Yankee fan responds, 'Good for you. In New York, we're taught to not piss on our hands.'"

My grandpa chuckled. I didn't.

Grandpa Kalb's grin disappeared. "What?" he said. "You don't like that joke?"

"No. I mean, yes," I corrected, not wanting to tip my hand. "I do. That's really funny."

"All right, well, the appropriate thing to do is laugh."

"Sorry," I said and then forced a laugh.

Grandpa Kalb just shook his head and then continued into the bathroom.

As soon as my grandpa was gone, my eyes jumped to his suitcase. I decided that if I couldn't convince him to go to the doctor, I would have to play one myself. At least that seemed like a good idea. I knew that I couldn't just force him to take his medicine, so I had already concluded that the best move would be to slip the meds into his next Mountain Dew. However, after sifting through Grandpa Kalb's stockpile of prescriptions for just a few seconds, I started to doubt my plan. Even if slipping a mickey in his Mountain Dew would work, I had no idea what I needed to give him. Only the Marinol was marked, and I couldn't remember the specific purpose of the other pills. From his brief explanation, I knew there was a delicate balance. I didn't want to risk giving him the wrong dose and have it not work or, even worse, create some lethal combination.

I tossed around a few other ideas, but none of my ideas were realistic options. The more I tried to come up with a solution, the more I realized that it wasn't a decision that I could make on my own. I needed help and there was really only one place where I could go to get it.

I grabbed the handle for the bedside phone and quickly punched the numbers.

"This is Dr. Lewis," my dad said as he answered his cell phone.

"Dad, I need your help," I whispered softly so Grandpa Kalb wouldn't hear.

"Jordan?" he said, his voice cracking.

Before I could say anything else, I heard my mom in the background. "Put it on speakerphone," she pleaded. My dad immediately obliged, and my mom continued in a clearer, but equally hurried, voice, "Jordan, honey, where are you? We've been waiting at Grandpa's since Thursday. We've been worried sick about you."

Hearing the worry in my mom's voice, combined with the knowledge that my parents had been able to survive, let alone exist, in the same room for three days, threw me for a loop. "Uh," I stuttered, momentarily forgetting what I was calling about before regaining my wits. "We're in New York. But that's not important. I need your help. I'm worried about Grandpa. He's really weak, and he's been going to the bathroom a lot."

"His blood sugar is probably spiking," my dad said.

"He's been drinking a ton of soda," I said.

"That's definitely not good for his diabetes."

"Has he been taking his medicine?" my mom asked.

"Not today," I said. "And I'm pretty sure he didn't take it all yesterday. He said he doesn't need to on Sunday."

"That's not true at all. Oh my god," my mom whimpered. I could hear her breathing begin to pick up.

"It's gonna be okay," my dad said to her, and then turned his attention back to me. "Listen, Jordan, I don't know what's going on with your grandpa, but this is very serious. We have a police officer with us right now, and he can get an ambulance sent to where you are. But you need to tell us exactly where you are."

"We're at the Days Inn by Yankee Stadium. In room 374." No sooner did I finish, than I heard the toilet flush. "He's coming. I need to go."

"Okay," my dad said. "Just stay where you are."

"I will."

"Good. We love you," my dad said, his voice cracking as he spoke.

I could hear my mom crying in the background. My eyes started to well up. "I love you too." I hung up the phone and was wiping my eyes when Grandpa Kalb exited the bathroom.

"What's up with you?" he said.

"Nothing," I said. "Just ... allergies. All this dust and stuff."

"Lucky you, we're getting out of here," Grandpa Kalb said and started for the door.

"No!" I shouted with way more enthusiasm that I'd intended. Grandpa Kalb stopped and glared at me suspiciously.

"I'd just rather stay here for a little while," I said.

"With all the dust and allergies?"

"In spite of them, yes. I've been driving so long, and we have plenty of time before the game starts. I just need to relax for a minute. Maybe five or ten or twenty."

"Too bad," Grandpa Kalb said. "There's too much to do. If you'd rather stay here, you can do that, but I've got plans."

I didn't want to leave, but I knew that, short of using force, there was no way I'd be able to keep my grandpa in the room. Using force was no guarantee either. I wasn't exactly a physical specimen, and my grandpa had already demonstrated enough old-man strength to keep me from getting to the cops earlier. Odds were that I wouldn't be able to stop him, and I'd only make him mad.

My best and only option was to go with him and alert the first police officer or paramedic that we saw. I spotted the notepad and pen lying on the nightstand next to the phone and got an idea. If he told me, I could write it down and send the ambulance to us.

"Well, where are we going?" I asked.

"It's a secret," Grandpa Kalb said.

"Just tell me."

"If I told you, it wouldn't be a secret." He smirked. "I'm hitting the road. You can come if you want to or you can stay if you want to." He opened the door and started outside.

"Wait!" I said, a last-ditch idea popping into my head. "I just thought of something."

"What now?" Grandpa Kalb asked, annoyed.

"Shouldn't we maybe leave the tickets here until we're going into the stadium? I mean … this seems like a rough neighborhood. We could easily get mugged and lose the tickets."

Grandpa Kalb considered my suggestion for a few seconds and then said, "That's actually not a terrible idea. We do have to pass by a couple dicey neighborhoods. And the Bronx sure ain't what it used to be."

"Exactly," I agreed as if I knew it to be true, which I didn't. "It's a shame."

"You got that right." Grandpa Kalb let the door close, retrieved his wallet and the tickets, and then slid the tickets into the second dresser drawer. "Now, we're good to go."

I reluctantly followed Grandpa Kalb out of the room, taking my time and hoping that, if I moved slow enough, we might meet the ambulance on our way out. We didn't. Nor did we cross paths with the ambulance or any law enforcement as we made our way down Melrose Avenue. I kept my eyes peeled at every intersection. About five blocks into our walk who-knew-where, I swore I heard the faint whine of a siren and stopped.

"Stop dragging ass," Grandpa Kalb shouted.

I tried to find the sound again, but it either hadn't existed or just blended into the other frenetic sounds of the city.

It wasn't until fifteen minutes later, when we made it to River Road and Yankee Stadium was right in front of us, that I finally saw my first cop.

22

I first saw the cop from about a hundred yards away from the River Road intersection as we flowed with the massive crowd of fans down 158th Street. The whole area was so packed with people, all sporting their best Yankees gear just like Grandpa Kalb, that it was pure luck that I even spotted the officer. I kept my eyes locked on him as we continued on a direct line toward his post. There was no way I was going to lose him in the crowd.

By the time we made it to River Road, which ran along the stadium and was even more congested than 158th Street, the officer was less than 50 yards away. I was silently praying that my grandpa wouldn't see him, and it seemed to be working too. But, just as I was starting to think that we might actually make it to the police officer, I heard Grandpa Kalb shout, "Hey! Where are you going?"

I turned to find that my grandpa had started up River Road. "Where are you going?" I said as I sidestepped around the rest of the people who were continuing to the stadium.

"Stan's," Grandpa Kalb said and pointed to the sign a few

doors up the road. "The best sports bar in the world. That's the surprise. We're going there for lunch."

"You need tickets, man?" a scalper asked Grandpa Kalb.

While my grandpa was distracted, I turned back to the officer and considered my options. I could make a dash for him and get his help. There was a chance it could work. Of course, I knew that, realistically, by the time we worked our way back against the flow of the crowd, the odds that my grandpa would've disappeared in the crowd were as close to one-hundred percent as you can get. My only other option was to try to flag down the officer from where I was. But, with that option, I knew the likelihood of the officer even seeing me in the crowd was low, and I'd still be alerting my grandpa and running the risk of him making a run for it.

I hadn't completely written off the second option when Grandpa Kalb, who had shooed away the scalper, said, "Stop screwing around. Let's go."

I sighed. I was so close, but there was nothing I could do. I couldn't risk it. I followed my grandpa inside Stan's, determined to take advantage of the next opportunity I had.

After we found a tiny empty spot in the corner of the packed bar, Grandpa Kalb flagged down a waitress and ordered a beer and a dozen chicken wings. I wasn't hungry, my stomach was too tied in knots to be, but I ordered a burger and fries, so as not to raise any red flags.

"Can you believe all those damn scalpers out there?" Grandpa Kalb said and shook his head. "Sons of bitches just try to rake you over the coals. Selling tickets for ten times face value ... it should be a crime. I mean, it is a crime. I'm just glad we already have tickets."

Grandpa Kalb continued his rant on scalpers while I scanned

the bar for any law enforcement or authority figure that might be able to help. After failing to find anyone who looked sober enough to help, I decided my best move would be to find a payphone and alert my parents so they could redirect the ambulance.

"Where's the bathroom?" I asked my grandpa, knowing that payphones tended to be right by bathrooms.

"Right there," he said, pointing to the door ten feet away and in clear view.

Sure enough, there was a payphone. Unfortunately, though, it was also in clear view. Which meant my original plan went down the toilet.

"Aren't you gonna go?" Grandpa Kalb said.

"Go where?" I said.

My grandpa looked at me like I was crazy. "The bathroom. Usually, when people ask where the bathroom is, it means they're gonna go."

"Oh, yeah. I am going. I just got distracted by all the people here. It's just so cool."

"You bet your ass it is."

"All right, well, I'm going to the bathroom." I got up from the booth and wove through the crowd. I stopped right by the payphone and turned back to my grandpa just in case he wasn't looking and I could make a quick call. I couldn't tell if he was actually watching me, but he was staring right in my direction. So, I gave up on the payphone completely and slipped into the men's room. As packed as the bar was, the bathroom was completely empty. I paced between the sink and stall, waiting for the next person to enter. It was part of my new plan. Instead of the payphone, I was hoping that maybe someone would let me borrow their cell.

Finally, after half a minute, the door opened, and a man who was almost as wide as he was tall and looked like someone from *The Sopranos* entered. "Excuse me," I said and put my hand out as I stepped in front of him. "Can I use your phone?"

Without saying a word, he grabbed me by the shirt and tossed me up against the tile wall so hard that I could feel my ribs getting ready to crack.

His fists pushing into my chest, I strained to speak, "I just—"

"Think I'm a goddamn idiot?" he growled. "I don't know what kinda scam you're trying to pull but pull that shit on someone else."

He let go of me, and I crumbled to the ground. I picked myself up and brushed off my clothes. As I hobbled out of the bathroom, I passed another guy who gave off a similar demeanor to the man who'd just assaulted me. Not looking to start a two-on-one fight, I thought better of asking to use his phone.

I did my best to hide my pain as I rejoined Grandpa Kalb in the corner. I didn't do as good of a job as I'd hoped. He looked me up and down and said, "That must've been a rough dump. You know you should never push too hard. That's how you get hemorrhoids. Those are a pain in the ass. Literally." Grandpa Kalb chuckled at his joke.

I faked a laugh and shielded my face as my friend from the bathroom passed by.

While we waited for our food and through the first half of our meal, Grandpa Kalb ran down the history of the bar and a few of the more memorable times he'd eaten at Stan's. He choked up a little toward the end of his story, recalling his last time coming to the restaurant: a date night he'd had with my grandma after her doctors informed them that her cancer was in remission—a position they'd reverse only a month later. After a moment of misty-eyed reminiscing, he wiped his face with his napkin and then returned to his chicken wings.

My eyes bounced back and forth from the clock behind the bar to my grandpa. The likelihood that the ambulance was still at the hotel was disappearing much faster than the wings on my grandpa's plate. I knew I needed to get him back there and fast.

"We should get going," I blurted.

"You've barely touched your food," Grandpa Kalb said.

I picked up my burger, took three large bites, and then, with my mouth still full, said, "That's all I can eat." I swallowed the barely chewed burger. "But I'd really like to get to the stadium so we can check out Monument Park." I figured my grandpa would want to hit up the outdoor museum that was located just beyond the left-center field wall and the two bullpens.

Grandpa Kalb grinned. "How do you know about Monument Park? I haven't mentioned it."

"I read about it in the paper this morning. I also read that it's only open before the game."

"That is correct. But don't you worry. It was already on the agenda. That was actually gonna be surprise number two." He glanced at the clock. "I guess the gate's been open for long enough now. The crowd should've died down a little. Just let me finish my beer and wings, pay the bill, and then we can go." He took a small sip from his half-empty beer.

I knew if he kept it up, we wouldn't be leaving for at least another twenty minutes. "We really should go right now," I said.

"Why are you in such a damn hurry?" Grandpa Kalb said and nibbled one of his wings. "You gotta enjoy the moment."

At first, I didn't have an answer and then the perfect answer came to me. It was just what I needed to trigger his old-man sensibilities. "Sorry. It's just that I realized that the cleaning staff was waiting in the hall on our way out," I said. "I know, they looked like nice ladies, but they were kind of hovering around like they were waiting for something. Like they were waiting for us to leave. And they obviously saw that you were wearing Yankees gear, so they have to know we're going to the game."

Grandpa Kalb's jaw went slack. So did his hand, which dropped the chicken wing on the table. "You're right. Screw the food. We need to go right now." A look of determined urgency swept across the old man's face. His hand shot up and shook wildly as he tried to flag the waitress.

After we paid the bill, I led the charge back to the hotel, moving at a brisk speed and doing my best to make sure Grandpa Kalb matched it. The meal had given him a boost of energy, as well as an added level of clarity, but it still wasn't enough to keep up with me.

"Jesus Christ, Jordan," Grandpa Kalb said, gasping for air. "I'm not as spry as I used to be. You might need to go ahead without me."

"No. We need to go together," I insisted and grabbed my grandpa by the arm to help him.

A few blocks later, with just a couple blocks left to go, I spotted the flicker of the ambulance and an assisting police car. I sighed inwardly, relieved that they were still there and that Grandpa Kalb would get the help he needed. Fueled by this knowledge, I picked up my pace and blew past my grandpa.

"We're almost there," I said. "We won't let them get the tickets." I made a few more strides and then stopped. I turned back to find my grandpa, fifteen feet behind and backing further away as he gazed at the lights ahead. "What are you waiting for?" I said, starting toward Grandpa Kalb.

"That's our hotel," he said, nodding his head. "I think they found us."

"You're just being paranoid. No one even knows we're here. They didn't find us."

"Yeah, they did. It's all my fault. After all the room service last night, I burned through so much cash that I had to use my credit card for the room. They must've put a trace on it."

"That's crazy. There's no way they would know that fast."

"We need to wait a minute. We need to wait until they leave."

"No. We can't. By then, our tickets could be gone. Come on. Let's go. Come on!" I grabbed his hand and tried to pull him with me. In doing so, I overplayed my hand and revealed my true intentions to my grandpa.

With surprising old-man strength, Grandpa Kalb ripped his hand free and cast a scowl in my direction that was so strong it sent chills down my body. "It wasn't me, it was you," he said through gritted teeth. "What the hell did you do?"

Busted, I did what anyone in my situation would've done: I lied. "I don't know what you're talking about," I said, feigning bewilderment. "I didn't do anything. But even if the cops are there for us, I'm sure they wouldn't even recognize us with our disguises anyway. We're Forrest Gump and Charlie Cash. So, let's get the tickets before the maids steal them."

"No!" Grandpa Kalb said firmly. "And stop lying to me. Stop trying to feed me your bullshit! You called the cops, didn't you?"

"I swear I didn't call the cops," I insisted. While it was the truth, my face must have betrayed the bigger lie because Grandpa Kalb didn't buy my innocence.

"Then what the hell did you do? Because you clearly did something."

Based on the rabid look in his eyes, I accepted the fact that I wasn't going to convince him that I didn't do anything and decided to switch to focusing on convincing him to do something. "Fine!" I said. "I admit it. I called my parents, okay? Now you stop lying to me!"

"You little shit," he said and shook his head. "My tickets are in there! I barely have any cash left. Definitely not enough for a ticket. How the hell am I supposed to get into the game?"

"Forget the damn game. You need to get to a hospital."

"That's the last place I need to go."

"No, it's not. Something is obviously wrong with you," I pleaded. "I don't know if it's because you skipped your meds, but you're not well. You could die."

"Yeah, I know," he said, his anger subsiding. "That's the goddamn point."

My grandpa's words hit me like a Mike Tyson punch to the gut, knocking the wind out of me. The possibility that he might be slowly killing himself hadn't even crossed my mind; yet, that had been his plan all along. Once it was revealed, it all made sense. It was the only reason he'd agreed to go on the trip. It was the reason he'd loaded up on all the junk food and stopped taking his medicine. It was also the reason he had refused to tell me what was wrong and why he had been fighting me so hard.

"You ... you can't do this," I stuttered. "That's not how it works."

"I don't give a damn how it works," he said. "It never works like it's supposed to anyway. It wasn't supposed to be like this. I'm not supposed to be here."

"What are you talking about?"

"I was three years older than your grandmother and men die younger. I was supposed to go first! There's nothing I can do to change that, but I'm not gonna wait around to get cancer or

something else, to go through the pain that most of my heroes
and your grandmother went through. To hell with that!"

"What about the pain you'll cause everyone else? What about
my mom? What about her?"

I could tell Grandpa Kalb was fighting to suppress any signs
of emotion as thoughts of the heartache he would cause my
mom danced around his head. He blocked most of them, but
even still there were cracks. "She's a strong woman," he said.
"She can take care of herself."

"Well," I said and then swallowed hard, "what about me?"

"What about you?" he said. "Three days ago, you wouldn't
have even cared if I died. The only thing you would've cared
about is how much money I was leaving you."

"Yeah," I agreed. "But a lot has changed in those three days."

"And even so, a lot hasn't," he sighed. It was clear his mind
was made up. I wouldn't be convincing him of anything.

"I'm not gonna let you do this," I said firmly.

"It's not your call."

"I don't care. I'm gonna go get the cops."

"Go for it."

Unlike before, there was no crowd to fight. That combined
with how winded my grandpa was, I was confident that I could
make it to the cops and get back to my grandpa before he even
made it a block. I started to sprint toward the hotel. I'd made it
maybe twenty yards when I heard an ear-splitting whistle. I
came to a skidding stop on the sidewalk and turned back to my
grandpa. He had one arm raised and was flagging down a cab.

The yellow and black checkered taxi came to a halt beside
Grandpa Kalb. "Last lesson I teach you is how to hail a cab," he
said as he opened the door. "You can still go to the cops if you
want, but they'll probably just take you into custody. And I guar-

antee they got better things to do than look for an old man like me."

"Don't go," I screamed. "Please."

Even from a distance, I could still see the single tear that broke away from his eye and rolled down his cheek. "Sorry," he said and wiped the tear. "I was gonna save my goodbye for the end of the game, but I guess I'll have to do it now. For what it's worth, the last few days really were the best I've had in the past three years. But I'm going out on my own terms, not someone else's." He clenched his fist. "I'm doing it my way."

I took off toward the cab, but Grandpa Kalb had already slipped inside and closed the door before I could get there. I pounded on the window with my fist as the vehicle started to make a U-turn. Grandpa Kalb averted his eyes, instructing the cabbie to keep driving. I smacked the trunk just before the taxi sped off and then watched it disappear down the street through blurry vision as tears streamed down my face.

I wiped my eyes with my sleeve and swallowed the clump of mucus that had pooled in the back of my throat. I turned to the cops, who were still waiting outside the hotel. I wasn't sure if Grandpa Kalb had just been trying to dissuade me from going to them or not. Regardless of what his true intentions were, I knew there was at least a small chance that he was right—that the police would just take me in and that would be that. I didn't want to take that risk. I knew there was only one way that I could guarantee at least one person was out there busting their hump—as my grandpa would say—and trying to help him: I had to go it alone.

23

I t was another twenty minutes before the police and ambulance finally packed up and drove away. Once they were gone, I snuck back into the hotel, pretending to scratch the side of my head with my hand to shield my face as I passed by the front desk.

Just to be extra safe, I took the stairs to the third floor. I made sure no one was watching before stepping out into the hall and then tiptoed toward the room. I retrieved the room key from my pocket, opened the door, and quickly slipped inside.

The place was a mess. The sheets were ripped off of the bed and Grandpa Kalb's suitcase had been emptied, the contents dumped on the floor. It was definitely not the work of the imaginary maids. The police had turned the place, probably searching for any information on our whereabouts. My thoughts immediately shifted to the tickets, my whole reason for returning. I jerked my head toward the dresser and discovered all the drawers opened. I took a deep breath and closed the top drawer to get a view inside of the second. In spite of my foolish hope that the tickets had gone unnoticed, they were gone. Something told me they weren't heading to an evidence locker either. I slammed the second drawer shut and then kicked the third, taking out my frustration on the shoddy furniture.

With no time to sulk, I recollected myself, ducked out of the room, bounded the stairs, and then exited the hotel. I raced toward the stadium, arms chugging and legs flailing. Having not been in the best of shape, my sprinting only lasted a few blocks before I was forced to switch to a fast-paced walk of fluctuating speeds.

Ten minutes later, I was back in front of the stadium. I scanned the still packed crowd that was gravitating toward the stadium gates, searching for both my grandpa and a scalper to buy a ticket from. I wasn't expecting to find my grandpa so easily, but I wasn't expecting to have such a hard time finding a scalper. A little over an hour early, the place had been flooded with them.

Finally, I saw the guy who'd bothered my grandpa outside of Stan's. He was hanging out with a few other guys that I swore I'd also seen selling tickets. I wove through the crowd, making my way to the group. When I eventually got to the group, I learned why they were just hanging out—they'd already unloaded all of their tickets. They said that almost all the scalpers were out and then pointed me in the direction of another group. I bounced around the scores of scalpers, but the story was the same for all of them.

After getting shot down by five more scalpers, I finally found one that still had a few nosebleed tickets left. "Hundred and fifty, Forrest," the scalper said with a grin.

"Okay," I sighed. I found my grandpa's rant replaying in my head. While I agreed with him even more at the moment, there was nothing I could do about it. I pulled out my wallet and retrieved the "emergencies only" debit card that my parents had given me and offered it to the scalper.

"Ha!" he shouted, laughing so hard he almost choked on his toothpick. "What do you think this is, Ticketmaster? It's straight cash, homey. That's all I take, and that's all I make."

"But I don't have cash."

"Then you also don't have a ticket."

"I really need it," I pleaded.

"You do?"

"Yes. More than anything."

The scalper considered this for a second and then grinned. "Why didn't you say that before? In that case, the price just went up to two hundred large."

"What? Why? That doesn't make any sense."

"Supply and demand. Never show your cards, Gump. Including your debit cards."

I wanted to roll my eyes. I wanted to regurgitate everything my grandpa has said about scalpers. But as much as I wanted to give him a piece of my mind, I wanted the ticket even more. "Fine," I said. It was still within the daily withdrawal maximum that my parents had set, and it still wasn't my money. "Where's the nearest bank?"

"There's an ATM about a block that way," he said, pointing away from the stadium.

"Okay," I said. "Just hold one ticket for me."

"Sure thing. Now, run Forrest, run!"

I shook my head at his shitty joke and then sprinted the block toward the standalone ATM. As I got closer, and the machine came into view, I was pumped to see that there wasn't a line. As I came to a stop in front of it, my excitement completely disappeared, and I found out why no one else was trying to get money. Taped on the front of the screen was a handwritten note that notified any would-be users that the ATM was empty.

I'd started to read the note again, just to make sure, when a random fan passing by patted me on the back and said, "Good luck getting cash. All the ATMs in the area are tapped out."

"Thanks," I muttered under my breath, turning to watch the fan continue into the merchandise and apparel store next to the ATM. As the door swung shut, I spotted the "credit cards accepted" just above the handle, and it gave me an idea.

I hurried inside and found someone waiting in line to buy a Derek Jeter jersey and a few other items. He looked mostly harmless, but I played it safe anyway as I approached him and then explained my deal: I would buy him $400 worth of Yankees apparel if he gave me $200 cash. After I confirmed that there were no strings, that I wasn't a cop, and that the debit card was from my parents and not stolen, he finally agreed. I paid for his jersey, a couple t-shirts, and a hat, and then took off with my two hundred dollars in hand.

I bolted back to my scalper friend, who had moved half a block further from the stadium and was negotiating with a couple. I quickly cut them off. "I. Got. The. Money," I said in between gulps of air as I approached.

"Really?" he said, more surprised than I was expecting.

"Yeah," I said and held out the cash.

The scalper just looked at it and shrugged. "Shit. I'm sorry, kid. I sold that ticket a couple minutes ago."

Not only did I lose the tickets, I lost my temper. "What the hell?" I screamed. "You said you would hold it!"

"Aw, man, you believed that? I didn't think you were actually serious. I already told you, I'm not Ticketmaster. I don't hold nothing."

"This is bullshit."

"Calm down," he said. "I feel bad about our miscommunication. I'll call some of my boys and see if I can find you something. I'll even try to hook you up and get you something for $150."

I sarcastically thanked the scalper, but even that was premature and undeserved, because he wasn't able to "hook me up" with anything. "Looks like everyone is out," he said after trying the last number from his list of scalper friends.

I shook my head and stormed toward the stadium. "Good luck, Gump," the scalper shouted out to me.

I was about to turn around and scream back something that would have probably gotten me beat up when an idea popped into my head. Instead of fighting my clean-cut image, there was a chance I could use it to my advantage, just like my grandpa had when he was my age.

I flexed my face to keep my eyes open as I approached the gate. The breeze and lack of blinking caused my tear ducts to turn on like timed sprinklers, watering my cheeks. I let the tears roll down my face and took short and fast breaths to wind myself. Once I was adequately worked up, I started screaming, "Dad? Dad?" and sprinted past the stadium entrance, my eyes manically searching as I ran.

My plan worked even better than I'd expected. I didn't make ten feet past the entrance when a muscular and tatted up, UFC-looking security guard called after me. "Hey, kid! Stop!"

I followed his orders, huffing my breath even harder as he jogged up to me.

"What's wrong?" the jacked guard asked.

My words flew from my mouth like they were shot out of a

cannon. "We were all together and now we're not and I don't know where they went or where they're going or what to do."

"Slow down, little bro. Just take a breath and tell me what happened."

I took a deep breath and then exhaled. I slowed my speech by taking big breaths between every five or so words. "I was with my dad," I said, my hands fidgeting. "And then I stopped to look at some hats that were for sale. And when I went to find my dad, he was gone. I don't know what I'm gonna do. I'm not from here, and I don't have a cell phone." I buried my head in my hands and started to whimper.

The guard patted my back. "It's okay. Just give me a second, and I'll figure this out."

"Thanks," I sniffled, still putting on a show.

I kept my head down and eavesdropped as the jacked security guard talked to his husky partner. The jacked guard said that he was going to take me to the main security office in case my dad showed up. His partner was skeptical, correctly assuming that my act was really just a scam.

"Look at the little guy," the jacked guard said. "He's clearly not from around the block."

"You're right about that," the husky guard agreed. "He couldn't have been in the city for more than a few hours, otherwise he would've been beaten up a few times already."

"Exactly."

"All right, fine," the husky guard conceded. "Just be quick. And grab me some nachos on your way back."

The jacked guard returned and told me to follow him. The husky guard eyeballed me as I passed through the turnstile. I closed my lids extra hard to squeeze out the last few tears from my eyes, and he turned back to the crowd and his job.

I followed the jacked guard through the packed stadium tunnel for a while, waiting for the perfect moment to make a break. When he noted that, "The security office is just up ahead," I realized that I couldn't wait for the perfect moment. I just had to settle for that moment.

"Thanks for your help," I said and then discreetly slipped away. I sprinted in the opposite direction, weaving through the crowd. I wasn't sure if the jacked guard was on my tail or not. Mostly, because I was too afraid to look back to confirm that he was. Plus, I knew that checking would only slow me down.

My answer came a little over five seconds later, when the jacked guard shouted, "Hey, kid! Get back here!"

By that point, I was far enough away that I was hidden by the dense crowd. Instead of just running—and losing steam quickly, like I knew I would—I used the crowd as a human shield and ducked into a small alcove, undetected. I stood completely still and hidden, watching the tunnel. A few seconds later, the jacked security guard flew past my hiding spot, barreling through the crowd like Reggie Jackson as he searched for me. I counted to twenty to make sure the coast was clear and then headed back in the original direction that the jacked guard had led me.

I stopped at the first souvenir stand I came across and used my two hundred dollars to buy a fitted hat, a Robinson Cano t-shirt jersey, and a pair of sweatpants that said Yankees up the side of one of the legs. I slipped into the nearby bathroom, went into the stall, and threw on my new clothes.

I dumped my old clothes in the trash and then checked myself out in the mirror. Finally, I didn't look like Forrest Gump anymore. I looked like everyone else, like a regular Yankees fan.

I did a quick scan of the bathroom to make sure my grandpa wasn't inside. Unfortunately, dumb luck hadn't magically led us to the same place, and he wasn't there. I started for the exit, passing a fan in his forties on my way out.

"Go Yankees!" he screamed and pumped his fist.

"Go Yankees!" I shouted back, pumping my fist too.

As I exited the bathroom, I spotted a closed-circuit TV hanging on the wall across the tunnel. It was broadcasting a shot of the field as they announced the lineups from years past. I watched as Yogi Berra jogged to the plate and then they panned across the stadium. Everyone was on their feet for a standing ovation. I knew that somewhere in that stadium shot was my grandpa. I also knew that the game was about to start very soon. That meant that I had nine innings, just twenty-seven Yankees' outs, to find him. I wouldn't stop until the last out.

"It ain't over till it's over," I said to myself and then took off down the tunnel.

24

As planned, my first stop was Monument Park; however, by the time I made it there, they had already closed the entrance and ushered out all the visitors. There were just a couple fans still hanging around the gates, but Grandpa Kalb was nowhere to be seen.

Through the closed, metal gate, I spotted the plaques that were attached to the old stadium and paid tribute to the Yankee greats. I also noted the six red granite slabs that stood off on their own. Each slab also had a plaque; they honored Ruth, Gehrig, DiMaggio, Mantle, and former manager Miller Huggins. The last slab was for the victims and heroes from the September 11th attacks. I allowed myself a moment to pay my respects before waving down the museum guard.

"Hey," I shouted after getting his attention. "I know you're closed, but you didn't happen to see an old guy in Yankees gear, did you?"

"Are you kidding me?" the museum guard chuckled. "I saw about a thousand old guys in Yankees gear."

I'd realized how stupid my question was even before the

museum guard reminded me. "The guy I'm looking for was wearing an old Yankees jacket—"

"You don't say?"

"I wasn't done," I said, trying not to let my annoyance show too much. "The jacket has a hot pink Y on the back."

"Actually, I do remember that guy!" the museum guard said. "He had a really bad dye job, like super jet-black hair, and he kept talking to himself."

"That's him! That's my grandpa. How long ago was he here?"

"Not that long. Just before we closed. So maybe about twenty minutes ago."

"You didn't happen to see which way he went, did you?"

"I think that way," he said and pointed to the right.

"Thanks," I said, but my words were drowned out by the eruption of cheers from everyone in attendance. I glanced at the field, where the players were jogging out to their positions. With the game about to start, I started my jog to what I expected was Grandpa Kalb's most likely next position: Section 39.

Section 39 was part of the right-field bleachers. The night that we dyed his hair, Grandpa Kalb had gone on and on for over a half-hour about the section and its famous occupants, a rabid group of fans affectionately referred to as the "Bleacher Creatures." Die-hards that went to every game, the Creatures were known for their rowdy cheers and chants. The most famous of their chants was the Roll Call, which was led by a guy named Bald Vinny. For Roll Call, Bald Vinny would shout a player's name, starting with the center fielder and then moving around the diamond, and then the rest of the Creatures would clap and chant the player's name until the player did something to acknowledge the section.

As I exited the tunnel to Section 39, the call had already commenced, and the Creatures were chanting, "Johnny Damon!" After a couple more chants, Johnny Damon dropped to a knee and pointed to the section with his glove and free hand.

I turned my attention back to the section and immediately found Bald Vinny. He was easy to spot. For starters, he was bald and wearing sunglasses, even though the sun had already set. He also had his hands cupped around his mouth to start the next chant and had at least ten people filming him, including someone who I swore was Spike Lee.

I scanned the group of people surrounding Bald Vinny as he got the "Nady" chant going for Xavier Nady, but I didn't see my grandpa. Vinny moved on to Bobby Abreu, and I expanded my search radius with equally poor results. The "Bobby" chants were interrupted by the crack of a bat, a fly ball hit right to Abreu. After he caught the ball, the chants started back up and then Bobby finally gave the Creature the wave they'd wanted.

As I made my way up the stairs and continued scanning all the faces in the section, I couldn't help but chant along. First, "Jason" for Jason Giambi, then "Robinson" for my favorite player, Robinson Cano, and then the full "Derek Jeter" for Derek Jeter, obviously. I finished searching the section just before the "A-Rod" chant started. There was still no sign of my grandpa.

I made one quick re-scan from the top of the steps while the Roll Call wrapped up with A-Rod. They skipped over the pitcher, Andy Pettitte, and the catcher, Jose Molina, as was the custom. As I hustled down the stairs toward the tunnel, the Creatures turned their attention to the box seats and were chanting, "Box seats suck!" followed by "We got Spike Lee," confirming that the guy filming actually was Spike Lee.

When I made it to the outfield stadium tunnel, I came to a

skidding, shoe-squeaking stop. My mind and heart were racing. I had no idea where to head next. Monument Park and Section 39 had seemed like the most likely places to find my grandpa early in the game. Knowing how much the history of the stadium meant to my grandpa, I decided I would start by checking all the sections that he had mentioned.

It took me almost three full innings to search the nosebleeds, where my grandpa had sat with his dad as a kid; behind home plate, where he'd gone on his honeymoon with my grandma; and the section along the third base line, which was where my grandpa's original tickets were for, where he had stated numerous times the best seats in the entire stadium were, and where he and my mom had been when the Yankees won the 1977 World Series.

While sprinting from spot to spot, I was able to keep up on the game thanks to the complaints of the fans that I passed in the tunnel. "At least they only got one run," was the general consensus after the top of the second inning. In the third inning, I heard a lot of insults directed at Melvin Mora and a couple optimists like Grandpa Kalb who insisted, "Don't worry. We'll get both runs back. We got plenty of time."

As I was flying up the stairs in the third base section after another unsuccessful search, I was stopped by a loud crack, followed by everyone in the stadium jumping to their feet. I turned and watched Johnny Damon's three-run homer fly all the way to right field and land not too far from the Bleacher Creatures. The Yankees had gotten the runs back and added one. I was hit with a flurry of high fives as I continued back up the stairs to the tunnel.

When I got to the tunnel, I really had no idea where to go next. I knew that my grandpa and his brother had roamed around the stadium when they were kids, so I decided to try that. I didn't roam just the concourse though. After remembering all of Grandpa Kalb's bathroom breaks, I decided that was probably a good place to look for him too.

I spent the next two innings in and out of just about every restroom in the entire stadium. There were way more than I'd even imagined. But, I guess it makes sense since fifty thousand people have to pee somewhere, right?

After doing some irreparable damage to my olfactory system during the first few bathrooms I checked, I started holding my breath before taking each restroom plunge. While it improved the overall sensory experience, or lack thereof, it also meant that sometimes, like a free diver exploring a contaminated coral reef, I had to come back up for air before making a second attempt to complete my search.

In all the time spent scouring the concourse and restrooms, I didn't get any closer to finding my grandpa. All I got was a lot of strange looks from the people who took breaks from handling their business at the trough urinals to watch the puffy-cheeked and red-faced teen tear through the room and then leave.

During what ended up being the last bathroom I checked, I ran into my friend from Stan's again. He was grabbing paper towels, and our eyes locked as I entered the bathroom. I immediately turned around and hauled ass out of there and down the tunnel. I decided that I was done with bathrooms, and I was done with running all over the place.

I had a pretty good feeling that I knew what my grandpa's final plan was. I was almost certain that he was going to try to run onto the field at the end of the game, assuming he made it that long. Instead of trying to find him while he was on the move, I decided to just hunker down on the third base line and let him come to me.

I plopped down on the stairway that pointed right at the third base bag and kept my eyes peeled for my grandpa. For two innings, I scoured each row of the nearby sections. And then, in the top of the eighth, with the Yankees comfortably ahead 7-3, I finally spotted my grandpa. He was just three sections over. The hot pink Y on the back of his satin jacket was unmistakable as he labored up the stairway.

I bounded up the stairs in my section, three and four steps at a time, and then raced around the tunnel toward the entrance for the section that my grandpa had been leaving. After working my way through a family of seven, who had unintentionally road-blocked me, I reached the entrance to my grandpa's section. Except, he wasn't there.

I recognized a few of the people entering the tunnel, they'd all been well behind my grandpa on the stairs, which meant that he had already made it inside. I whipped my head and quickly found him about twenty yards away, his too-black head of hair bobbing through the crowd as he approached the entrance to the restroom.

I darted toward him, caught up quickly, and grabbed his arm. "This ends right now," I said and whipped him around.

25

"What the hell are you talking about, kid?" grumbled the old man who was most definitely not my grandpa. Discovering that the person I was certain was my grandpa was really just some random old man made me momentarily lose my train of thought. "Uh," I stuttered.

"Let go of me before I call the cops," the old man said and jerked his arm free. In the process, his jacket opened up, and I noticed that the jersey he was wearing under was the same Yogi jersey that my grandpa had, which jogged my memory.

"The coat and jersey," I said, "where'd you get them?"

"From the store," he scowled and then started back toward the restroom.

"You're lying. The Y on the back is colored just like the one on my grandpa's jacket. That is my grandpa's."

The old man stopped and turned back around. His face softened and so did his tone. "That was your grandpa?"

"Yeah, and he's really sick. He's gonna die if I don't find him."

"I didn't know that," the man said, remorseful. "Honestly, I just thought he was on the sauce. He came up to me and asked me if I was a Yogi fan. I said, 'Damn, straight,' and then he handed me his jacket and jersey and said I could have them for free. Who even does that? I couldn't say no."

"When was this? Where was this? What was he wearing?" I fired off my questions rapidly, much too fast for the old man.

"Slow down," he said, his face scrunched. "One question at a time."

"When was this?" I said.

"It was right around the beginning of the game."

"Where was this?"

"Outside of the restroom by third base."

"What was he wearing?"

"A Cano t-shirt, same as you. He also had one of the classic pinstripe hats on." He pointed to a man in the crowd wearing the same off-white hat with pinstripes and a navy bill. "It looked really sharp."

I replayed my memory of scanning the third base stands in the second inning. I imagined the disguised version of my grandpa in the middle of a raucous pack of people and cheering along. While indistinguishable to me before, he now stood out of the crowd, popping off the page like Waldo after you find him and his red-striped sweater. I remembered seeing the hat, the jersey, and the hair sitting in the front row, the first seat in from the aisle. For a split second, I thought that it might have been my grandpa—the hair and the build were the same—but I'd quickly convinced myself it wasn't because of the clothes. I'd fallen victim to one of his clothes tricks once again.

I didn't know if my grandpa was still in the same seat, but I knew there was a chance he was. "Thanks," I said and then took off down the tunnel.

"You're welcome," the old man shouted after me. "And good luck."

Thanks to the Orioles pitcher only needing ten pitches to put the Yankees down in order, by the time I made it out of the small tunnel to the seating area, the bottom of the eighth inning was already over. I sprinted down the steps toward the seat where I'd last seen my grandpa. But, when I got there, there was some guy in his mid-40s in the seat.

"Where's the guy that was sitting here earlier?" I asked.

"I don't know," the mid-40s guy said. "He was standing on the stairs and he looked exhausted, so I told him he could have my seat for a little."

"When did he leave?"

"Right before the middle of the fifth."

As I was about to ask another question, "Enter Sandman" began to blast over the stadium's speakers. The announcer introduced Mariano Rivera, and everyone in the stadium, including the section I was trying to search, stood up and cheered. Camera bulbs flashed from all over the stands, washing out the crowd and making it impossible to locate my grandpa, let alone anyone. The whole stadium started chanting "Mari-ano."

Once the bulbs stopped flashing and my eyes readjusted, I returned to scanning the stands. Even though my grandpa had left a few innings earlier, I was certain he would be back. I knew this was where it would end. The only way Grandpa Kalb was going to step foot on the field was by going through me first, and there was no way I was going to let that happen.

"Where the hell are you?" I thought to myself as my eyes frantically hunted for Grandpa Kalb's pinstripe hat. I spotted a few matching caps but none of them were hiding the head of my grandpa.

Mariano made quick work of the first two hitters, retiring them on just seven pitches. In less time than it would take the wave to travel around the stadium, the Orioles were down to their last out—and so was I.

I started to think that maybe my grandpa wasn't coming. Maybe I'd guessed wrong about his final plan. Or, even worse, that maybe something had already happened to him. Maybe I was already too late. The only thing that kept my "maybes" from getting even more out of control was the cheering from all the fans, which was so loud that it could have drowned out a jet engine.

Before the potential last batter stepped up to the plate, the Yankees replaced Derek Jeter in the field. The already raucous crowd roared, cheering so loud that I could feel my eardrums vibrating. As I watched Jeter jog off the field, I got a strange feeling, the kind you get after you hand in a test and then realize that you answered one of the questions incorrectly, and only then does the actual answer pop into your head.

My thoughts flashed back to the business center at the Courtyard Marriott outside of Rocky Mount, North Carolina and watching the Reggie Jackson YouTube video. As the video replayed in my mind, I vividly remembered Reggie running toward the dugout. I could also envision my grandpa and mom running away from the same spot that Reggie was running toward. In spite of my grandpa's affinity for the third base seats, that wasn't where he and my mom had run onto the field from. It was the same spot that Jeter had just run to; it was the home dugout. It hit me like a Louisville slugger: I was on the wrong side of the stadium.

I gazed to the left of Derek Jeter, who had popped out of the dugout in response to the whole stadium chanting his name and demanding an encore. In the front row of the stands, sporting a pinstripe hat and supporting himself with both hands on the railing while everyone around him clapped, was my grandpa.

I shot up the stairs, making it to the ramp just as Mariano recorded the third out of the inning and final out of the game. "New York, New York," began blaring from the speakers. While everyone in the crowd was still standing and cheering and having the time of their lives, I was sprinting my ass off to get to my grandpa before he made his move for the field, a move that would cost him his.

As I reached the empty tunnel, I glanced at the closed-circuit TV. It not only showed the team lining up to shake hands, but it also showed the hundreds of cops jogging in from the outfield. While some were on foot and others were on horses, they all had guns and tasers attached to their hips. With Grandpa Kalb in such delicate shape, I had no doubt that either would be enough to deliver a lethal blow.

I didn't let my fatigue or the aches and pains that consumed my whole body slow me down as I barreled through the empty tunnel. On another TV, I caught Derek Jeter and the rest of the team making their way out to the mound, surrounded by cameras. Jeter's voice echoed throughout the stadium as he spoke into a microphone.

"For all of us up here," Jeter said, "it's a huge honor to put this uniform on every day and come out here and play. And every member of this organization, past and present, has been calling this place home for eighty-five years. There's a lot of tradition, a lot of history, and a lot of memories. Now the great thing about memories is you're able to pass it along from generation to generation. And although things are going to change next year, we're going to move across the street, there are a few things with the New York Yankees that never change—its pride, its tradition, and most of all, we have the greatest fans in the world."

As the stadium erupted in applause, I spotted the entrance to the first base section just thirty feet up ahead. I didn't slow down one bit. Instead, I used a move that Grandpa Kalb had taught me during his late-night lesson on base running. I bowed out to the right just a little and then made a curved left, like runner rounding first base and going for a double.

I exploded out of the tunnel ramp and back into the open stadium, just as the crowd was quieting down. I vaulted down the steps while Jeter continued his speech. "And we are relying on you to take the memories from this stadium, add them to the new memories that come at the new Yankee Stadium, and continue to pass them on from generation to generation. So, on behalf of the entire organization, we just want to take this moment to salute you, the greatest fans in the world." The crowd saved their most boisterous applause for this moment.

I reached the bottom of the steps just as the team was starting to leave the mound and heading toward left field. "New York, New York" cranked through the speakers once more. Only twenty feet of stadium seating separated my grandpa and me. As I struggled to catch my breath, I watched my grandpa, a huge smile on his face, have a conversation with an imaginary person. While I'd learn later that hallucinations were one of the symptoms of extreme Hyperosmolar Hyperglycemic Nonketotic Syndrome, which my grandpa had self-induced with his diet and skipping his medicine, I knew at that moment that he was talking to my mom. Grandpa Kalb tightened his grip on the railing, preparing to make his move.

"Stop!" I screamed, using everything left in my lungs and praying it was loud enough to carry over the commotion.

Thankfully, it was. Grandpa Kalb turned, still beaming. "How'd you get in here?" he shouted back.

"Fake tears and a story about being lost from my dad."

"I'll be damned." He smiled even wider. "Nice to know some things haven't changed. I had to take the goddamn taxi to five ATMs just to collect enough cash for the privilege of getting ripped off by a scalper."

"I got screwed over by one too."

"They really are the worst," he said and nodded. "I hope you enjoyed the game."

"Not for even a second," I said. "I was too busy looking for you."

"I'm sorry to hear," Grandpa Kalb said. "Now that you found me, you wanna join your mother and I on our race to the mound?"

"That's not happening. I'm taking you to the hospital."

Grandpa Kalb glanced down to where his hallucination of my mom was and chuckled. He turned his gaze back to me. "First, you gotta catch me," he said with a smirk and then wiggled his eyebrows.

"No!" I screamed, but it was too late. The old man had clearly saved whatever energy he had left for this moment. He leaped over the short fence with surprising ease and then sprinted toward the front line of police.

Everyone in the stadium started cheering again, as they saw my grandpa take off on the field.

I didn't think about what might happen if I joined him. I didn't have the luxury. I just reacted, hopping the fence and chasing after my grandpa.

Grandpa Kalb lowered his shoulder and knocked two cops to the side, clearing a hole for him—and then a second later for me —to run through. He did a juke move around the second line of cops, and I followed his lead.

Grandpa Kalb leaped over the chalked first base line, which he'd previously told me was unlucky to touch, and was on his way to the mound when a policeman on a horse skidded to a stop just in front of the mound, cutting him off.

"Stop or we'll have to tase you!" the policeman shouted.

"Change of plans," Grandpa Kalb yelled back to me as he veered to the right. "We're going to second!"

I immediately changed my course and was only a few feet from my grandpa when I spotted another policeman on a horse, galloping toward my grandpa. The officer had his stun gun leveled and aimed at my grandpa. I found another gear that I'd never used or knew existed and blew past my grandpa. As the electric tentacles exploded from the policeman's gun and in Grandpa Kalb's direction, I dove in front of my grandpa, laying out like Jeter trying to rob a liner up the middle.

26

Outside of the groin or face, the nipple is definitely the worst place to have a stun gun probe latch onto. It's one of the most sensitive parts of the body, and it's also where the cop hit me. Any thoughts that I'd had before the direct shot, instantly disappeared. They were replaced by one thought: the intolerable pain I was experiencing. I convulsed on the field like a souvenir bobblehead in an earthquake.

When the current finally ceased coursing through me, I had a brief moment to relax and enjoy the sweet smell of the infield grass, which was even nicer than I could've imagined. My pleasant moment of relaxation on the turf was much shorter than I would've liked.

Just a few seconds later, a hand grabbed my shoulder. I glanced up from the ground, hoping to find Grandpa Kalb. What I found instead was a snarling policeman with beet-red cheeks and hair to match. He drove his knee into the middle of my back and then went for my arms. It didn't take them long for them to restrain me. One, because I was a relatively small guy, and two, because I knew better than to try to fight with a cop, let alone seven. They threw a plastic zip tie around my wrists, yanked me up from the ground, and started to drag me away.

"Be careful with my grandpa!" I ordered the officers, as if I held any authority.

"Worry about yourself," one of the cops said. "You're in some deep shit."

"You don't understand," I said. "He's sick. He needs a doctor."

The cop just shoved me forward.

I glanced to my left and then right and realized that I was the only one being taken away. I wrenched my head as hard as I could, almost twisting a full 180 degrees, and for the briefest second caught a glimpse of my grandpa. He was lying on his back, unconscious, with two officers kneeling beside him. One officer was removing the stun gun probe, which was clamped to his chest. The other held two fingers to Grandpa Kalb's neck, checking his pulse. The last thing I noted before my head was snapped back around was my grandpa's eyes, which were open and rolled back.

I KNEW the news about my grandpa had to be bad when they didn't load me up to go to the regular police holding cell like they were doing with the other hooligans they'd detained. Instead, one of the officers, Lieutenant Daniels, drove me to the hospital in a squad car. Lieutenant Daniels refused to give me any information about Grandpa Kalb. He just put me in regular cuffs and then locked me to a chair in a hospital hallway.

Every once in a while, someone would pass by, a nurse or doctor or visitor, and I'd ask about my grandpa. Every time, they'd just give me the silent treatment. Then, finally, after three hours—that felt like twelve—I received something much better than the customary phone call that they grant every arrestee: My parents, escorted by Lieutenant Daniels, stepped out of the elevator halfway down the hall from where I was constrained. It turned out that, after I'd called them from the hotel, they'd hopped on the first flight out of Fort Myers. My eyes immediately welled up when I spotted my parents. "Mom? Dad?"

My voice was like a starting pistol in my mom's brain. She took off, sprinting down the hall toward me. She nearly tackled me as she wrapped me up in her arms and squeezed.

"Oh my God," she said. "We were so worried about you."

"Don't you ever scare us like that again," my dad said as he got in on the group hug.

"I won't," I said, tears streaming down my face. "I promise. I'm so sorry."

My parents matched my tears and squeezed me a couple more times.

"We're just glad you're safe," my mom said as she wiped her eyes.

"Although, I hardly recognize you," my dad said. "You look like you've changed a lot. I also never knew you were a Yankee fan."

"I am now," I said with a smile. My smile disappeared as I remembered Grandpa Kalb. "Where's Grandpa? Is he okay?"

"We don't know," my mom said, welling up again. "We still have to talk to his doctor."

My parents signed my release forms and then we made our way toward Grandpa Kalb's hospital room. When we arrived at the room, his doctor, Dr. Hirsch, was just finishing checking on him. My mom slowed to a near halt when she saw the doctor.

"It's gonna be all right," my dad said, putting his hand on my mom's back to comfort her.

"Yeah," I agreed and did the same.

My mom smiled weakly.

Dr. Hirsch made a few notes on Grandpa Kalb's chart and then returned it to the wall slot. She caught us making our tentative approach and said, "You must be the family."

"How is he?" my mom asked, bracing for the worst possible news.

"Stable," Dr. Hirsch said, "which is good."

"Is he going to be all right?"

"It's too early to tell."

My mom broke down. My dad and I quickly tightened our grips to help keep her upright.

Dr. Hirsch gave my mom a moment to recollect herself before continuing. "We're giving him fluids and insulin. But his blood sugar was so high that his body was minutes from shutting down even without the stun gun, which only exacerbated the trauma to his internal organs. We might not know for a few hours, maybe even a few days, if he's going to pull out of the coma. It's gonna come down to how much his body wants to fight."

We all thanked Dr. Hirsh and then she left to continue her rounds. My mom was still hesitant to see Grandpa Kalb in his current state, so my dad went in the room first, and I followed him. The room had a sterile smell, and it was completely silent, except for the soft, rhythmic beeping from the heart monitor. Grandpa Kalb appeared lifeless in his hospital bed. Tubes and wires, hooked up to all sorts of machines, were attached to every extremity. He looked like he was in worse shape than his friend Walter.

After a short moment, my mom joined us. "Oh my god," she exclaimed. "What happened to his hair? Is that normal?"

"I don't think so," my dad said.

"What could cause that?"

"It's Just For Men," I said. "We dyed it." Both of my parents shot me strange looks. "I can explain later."

"It looks terrible," my mom said, laughing through her pain.

My dad and I shared equally constrained chuckles as we lined up along Grandpa Kalb's bed.

My mom leaned in and kissed her father on the forehead and then made the sign of the cross where she kissed, just like he'd done to her when she'd dropped me off. A tear rolled down her cheek and landed on Grandpa Kalb's nose. My mom wiped it with her sleeve and sighed. "I don't tell you this as much as I should," she said, "but I couldn't have asked for a better father. I don't know where I'd be without you. I just wish I would've known how much you were suffering, so I could've been there for you the way you were always there for me."

"Come on, Grandpa," I said as I grabbed his hand, being extra careful to make sure I didn't interfere with the heart monitor clipped to his index finger. "Right now, you're down a lot of runs. Probably behind in the count too. Maybe even down to your last out. But what would Yogi say? You know he'd say that it ain't over till it's over."

"Don't let it be over," my mom insisted, tears streaming down her face. "I still need you."

"Me too," I agreed, my own ocular floodgates open.

"We all do," my dad said. He rested his hand on Grandpa Kalb's shin and gently squeezed.

"I know you can hear us," I sobbed. "We all need you. We all need you to fight."

"We do," my mom whimpered. "If you fight this and win, like I know you can, you can forget weekly dinners. Because I want nightly dinners. I want you to move in with me."

"Yeah. And we can watch the Yankees together, every single game. And we'll get to watch them win the World Series together. Probably not this season, but real soon they will. They'll win it all. Number 27. You don't want to miss that, do you?"

I'd be lying if I said I was expecting a response from my grandpa, but that didn't stop me from getting one. It was very subtle, just a gentle twitch of his hand. That was all I needed for spirits to lift. "He squeezed my hand!" I shouted. "I felt it."

My mom grabbed her father's other hand and held it tightly. "Don't give up, Dad," she urged. "Listen to me. Please, don't give up."

27

A little over eleven years later, as I rush to get to my parents' house in time for the start of Game 7 of the World Series, the deciding game between the Washington Nationals and Houston Astros, I can't help but think about the crazy road trip and the last game at Yankee Stadium.

A lot has changed since then. We didn't just pick up and leave the hospital the next morning as one big, happy family. Grandpa Kalb didn't even fully come to for another 36 hours. After that, it was a few more days before he was finally off all the machines and the doctors started to say that it looked like he was going to be okay. In total, he spent just under three weeks in the hospital and left with twice the number of prescriptions that he'd had before the trip. All of his doctors were adamant that, after the damage he'd done, he wouldn't survive another slip up.

My mom was determined to make sure that there wasn't even the slightest chance of another slip happening. As soon as Grandpa Kalb returned to Florida, she stuck to her word and moved him out of Punta Gorda Gardens and into the upstairs bedroom next to mine. Grandpa Kalb and I turned his new room into a shrine to my grandma and the Yankees.

Every morning, my mom sees to it that Grandpa Kalb takes his medicine. And if, for some reason, she's out of town, she texts me at 7 a.m. on the dot to remind me to remind him. Most of the time though, Grandpa Kalb has already popped his pills before the reminder and just replies, "I'm one step ahead of you."

Once Grandpa Kalb was really back on his feet, the first thing he did was head down to the local Buick dealership. They didn't take him seriously at first, especially after he told them that he'd probably need a few weeks to pass a drug test, but they gave him a job anyway. Five months later, he was already the top salesperson on the lot.

Every day after work, I'd ask him if he sold any cars.

And he would always give me the same response, "Didn't need to. Everyone knows Buicks sell themselves. I'm just the middleman."

Like my mom, I also stuck to my word, and Grandpa Kalb and I have watched almost every Yankees' game together. For the four years that I was away at college and couldn't be at home for the beginning of the season or end of the season games, we kept our tradition alive by talking on speakerphone while simultaneously watching from our respective locations. My college roommates weren't fans of my viewing habits or my cheering, but they learned to live with it.

My first year as a full-on fan, and the first year in the new stadium, couldn't have gone better. The Yankees won the World Series in six games—thanks, in part, I think, to Grandpa Kalb and my rally shirts and shirtless rallies. The Yankees clinched at home, beating the Phillies 7-3, the same score as the last game at the old Yankee Stadium. Andy Pettitte was even on the mound again. In both games, he gave up three runs and struck out three batters, and as any good Yankees fan knows, three was Babe Ruth's number.

Grandpa Kalb and I would've loved to go to the final World Series game or even any game since; however, as proof that actions do have consequences, the lifetime ban we received for running onto the field prevents us from getting within a thousand feet of the stadium. Thankfully, Stan's is just over a thousand feet away, so we were able to go there for my grandpa's 90th birthday. I'm crossing my fingers that a well-written letter and maybe congressional connection might eventually get the ban lifted. It would be nice to take Grandpa Kalb to the new stadium for his 95th birthday. I still have a few years to figure something out.

During my time on the run, my parents realized two things: one, how much pain they were putting me through, and two, that they could communicate a lot better when they weren't yelling at each other. The latter helped open the lines of communication and got them talking again, like civil human beings. They still went through with their divorce, because that's what they'd decided and that's what they were certain the other wanted.

For the first year and a half after the divorce, they kept their interactions limited to the occasional cordial conversation. And then, as if they'd coordinated it, they both started to communicate through me. My dad would ask me how my mom was doing. My mom would ask the same and if my dad was seeing anyone. I would tell her that he wasn't seeing anyone and that he asked me about her too. My mom would say that was interesting, which I would then relay to my dad when he asked me again. Eventually, I grew tired of all the questions and being in the middle and told them just to ask each other out already. Of course, because parents, despite their masquerading, are only slightly more rational than teens, they didn't listen to my advice.

It was another six months before they both realized that their jobs weren't enough, that they weren't happy alone, and that they missed being together. Even then, it was still another couple of months after that before they put aside their pride and finally acted on their feelings. It's actually a really funny story and not unlike Grandpa Kalb's.

The day my mom decided that she was tired of waiting for my dad to make a move and was going to just tell him how she felt, she drove to his condo right after work, except he wasn't there. She called his phone, but it just went straight to voicemail. When she arrived home, she was in a terrible mood and started complaining to me about my dad and how she'd finally gone over to talk to him; however, since he wasn't there, it clearly wasn't meant to be.

After my mom was done venting, I explained to her why my dad wasn't at his condo. He had actually just been over at the house with the intention of asking her out. When she'd called him, it only went to voicemail because he had been calling her. My mom called my dad again, and they made plans to go on their second first date.

My parents took their time rebuilding their romantic relationship. They wanted to make sure their foundation was firm so it couldn't fail again. Without prompting from the other, they both even chose to make sacrifices. My dad consolidated his surgery schedule and cut back on his lecturing, and my mom decided to forgo her next re-election bid and return to private practice, with more reasonable hours and a schedule that she set, of course.

They really made each other their number one priority—I was a close second, which is how it should be—and after two years of dating, they were remarried.

There really is something surreal about seeing your mom get escorted down the aisle by your grandpa on her way to marry your dad ... for the second time. Grandpa Kalb said it was déjà vu all over again. I think Yogi would've agreed.

Speaking of Yogi, on September 22, 2015, he passed away in his sleep from natural causes. I'm convinced the causes had to have been supernatural, because that's what Yogi was. His death came 69 years to the day after he made his debut in the majors and seven years and one day after the last game at the old stadium. He was 90 years young. Grandpa Kalb and I spent the day trading Yogi-isms like we had in the car, except this time, I had a few of my own. Here's one: When you come to a fork in the road, take it. That one is definitely in my top ten. Every time I say it, I can't help but smile, no matter how I'm feeling at the time.

As for winning Grace back, it was a lot easier than I'd expected it would be. I didn't really have to do anything except check my phone. When I got home, I had over a hundred unread messages from her. "Sorry" and "It's over" we just quick texts sent out of order and referring to the fact that her mother's meeting was over and that shouldn't text anymore. That was the third message. I won't bore you with the rest of the messages, but the gist was how much she missed me and how she hoped I was safe, since word of my jailbreak had spread quickly throughout school. That misunderstanding is a big part of the reason why I maintain that texting is the worst way to have an actual conversation with someone.

Winning over Grace's parents was just as easy and was also

included toward the end of her novel-length string of messages. Before I'd even gotten back, she admitted to her parents that the marijuana was hers and that I'd just taken the blame for her. While they slightly questioned my intelligence for taking the fall, they respected the lengths that I was willing to go to protect their daughter. Grace also told them about my road trip, which scored me even more points since Korean culture is really big on respecting their elders. I can't argue with them on that.

The cherry on top was when I finally met Mr. and Mrs. Kwon —I showed up to their house with my buzz and a nice shirt and tie, which my grandpa picked out for me—and it came up that Grandpa Kalb had fought in the Korean War. After they heard that, I swear they would've given me permission to marry Grace right then if I would've asked. Her dad even made the same joke about maybe knowing my grandpa, which I think proves that no matter our differences—whether race, religion, or whatever— we're all human, and we're all just a few years from developing a really corny sense of humor.

The review board at Fort Myers Prep wasn't as lenient as the Kwons. Despite my mom's impassioned defense, I was dishonorably discharged. Only after I transferred to the nearby public school did I realize how good I'd had it. However, I made the best of it anyway, turning shit into hits. I tried out for the baseball team in the spring and surprisingly didn't get cut. While my batting skills left something to be desired, I ended up being the top pinch runner, thanks to that extra gear I'd found chasing Grandpa Kalb. Grandpa, Mom, Dad, and Grace went to every game.

Derek and I made up too. Which is to say, I apologized for being a complete dick to him and to his parents. He apologized for ratting on us, but I told him that I deserved it. Plus, who knows what direction my life would've taken if he hadn't. I can say with full confidence that I would've never become so close to my grandpa if he hadn't. I still go over to Derek's house for dinner when he's back in town, and I always say please, even though the rest of his family doesn't anymore.

Grace and I studied together almost every day after school, and we hung out with the rest of the crew on the weekends. Billy decided that I was now a "jock goth" since I really only wore Yankees clothes from there on out, and I bored the group to death talking about the Yankees. My "Hair Jordan" nickname stuck too, both for my new buzz cut, which I kept since Grace surprisingly liked it, and because of my jock goth status. Grace stopped dressing goth junior year anyway, but she kept the perky part, which is great because that's still one of my favorite things about her.

When college came around, Grace and I made our first of many big sacrifices. Since we didn't get into the same school, we both agreed to go to schools that were lower on our lists so that we could at least be in the same city. After college, we entertained the idea of moving to New York, but then I learned that most young professionals in the city work so much that they don't even have time to watch the Yankees or really do anything else, which kind of defeats the purpose and made returning to Fort Myers and our families an easy call.

Probably the most surprising change though, even more so than my parents getting back together, was that my grandpa and I picked up a second favorite team: the Washington Nationals. We weren't trying to like them—even though plenty of people think it's acceptable to have a favorite American League and National League team—that wasn't our plan at all, but we couldn't help it. For starters, they were playing the team that knocked out the Yankees. But, even more than that, the Nationals embodied the Yogi spirit of not giving up until the game was over as much as any team ever. They even had their own rallying cry: Stay in the Fight.

Staying in the fight was what they had done all year, overcoming a 19-31 start to the season and fighting all the way back to make the playoffs as the wild card. They didn't quit during the regular season, and they didn't quit in the playoffs either. Going into Game 7, they had already faced elimination four times and had come from behind to win all four, including two rallys that started in the eighth inning.

Grandpa Kalb has been swearing that Game 7 is going to be the best game of the series yet, and I totally agree. As if being the deciding game isn't enough, it's also a matchup between Max Scherzer and Zack Greinke, two former Cy Young winners, and just three days earlier Scherzer was scratched from his Game 5 start because of neck spasm.

I'm still five minutes out when my phone buzzes. I wait till I hit the next red light to check it. It's a message from my grandpa, letting me know the game is starting and asking where I am. I type *Be there soon* and hit send just as the light turns green. I toss my phone onto the passenger seat and punch the gas.

"You missed the whole first inning," Grandpa Kalb says after I finally make it to my parents and join him on the couch.

"It's not my fault. I had to pick something up," I say and retrieve the ring box from my pocket, pop the lid, and hand it to my grandpa. "It wasn't supposed to be ready until next week, but it came early."

"Yikes," Grandpa Kalb says and pretends to struggle to hold the box. "That's a big rock."

I shake my head, smile, and take the box back.

"When are you talking to her dad?" Grandpa Kalb asks.

"We're going to dinner tomorrow," I say and slide the box into my pocket.

"Good getting his approval is important. Your dad never did that. That's probably why they got divorced the first time."

"Probably," I say as the commercials end and the game starts back up. "So, what did I miss?"

"Not much. Greinke looked good, too good. He only needed eight pitches to put down the side in order."

"What about Mad Max?"

"He got them out in order, but you can tell he doesn't have his best stuff. He's really gonna need to battle tonight."

For the next four innings, Max Scherzer does just that, getting into trouble but making the big pitches when he needs to and limiting the damage to just two runs. In his last inning, Max escapes a bases-loaded jam by getting a huge swinging strikeout.

While Max battles, Greinke coasts. His performance is nothing short of dominant, not just with his pitches but also with his glove. He's all over the infield making one spectacular play after another.

"He could go the whole damn game," Grandpa Kalb says as Greinke strikes out Trea Turner to end the sixth on just this 67th pitch.

"We'll see about the next inning," I say. "The Nats don't even like to get started until the seventh inning."

After Patrick Corbin works around a leadoff single by getting a strikeout and a double play, Adam Eaton grounds out to start the seventh, and I start to think that maybe this might not be the Nationals inning after all. Those thoughts change just two pitches later, when Anthony Rendon destroys Greinke's changeup and sends it flying into the left field stands.

"There it is!" I shout and jump out of my chair. "We have ourselves a game."

The next batter, Juan Soto, draws a five-pitch walk and then Greinke gets pulled from the game. "So much for pitching the whole game," Grandpa Kalb says.

"I'm not complaining," I say as Howie Kendrick takes a few cuts from the on-deck circle.

"Me either. You sure don't need to tell these Nats that it ain't over till it's over."

"That's for sure. They're in it until the last out."

"So am I," Grandpa Kalb says.

I turn to my grandpa and smile. "Thank God for that."

Grandpa Kalb grabs my hand and gives it a squeeze. I squeeze his hand back, and then we both turn to the TV and inch a little closer to the edge of our seats, waiting to see what kind of magic Howie has hidden in his bat.

THANK YOU

Thank you so much for reading *The Last Out*. I hope that you connected with the characters and enjoyed reading it as much as I enjoyed writing it.

As a sign of my appreciation, I want to offer the chance to join my Readers Group. Members receive free e-books, sneak peeks, and exclusive content, including the **first 50 pages** of every new book published by Wet Bandit Books.

Additionally, Readers Group members may also be selected to join my Advance Reader Team and receive full copies of all of my books prior to their release.

To join my Readers Group, visit my website:

www.matthewsullivanwriter.com/lastout

ABOUT THE AUTHOR

Matthew Sullivan is an author and screenwriter who found his calling after a yearlong battle with cancer. He specializes in coming-of-age stories that are humorous and heartwarming and focus on themes of empathy, empowerment, and human connection.

In his fifteen years as a writer, Matthew has sold several television and film projects, with one making it to the big screen, and has released three novels, with three more coming in 2020. The second oldest of seven children, Matthew was born in the suburbs of Washington, D.C. and raised there and in central Minnesota.

He currently lives in Scottsdale, AZ with his amazing wife and two young daughters.

facebook.com/matthewsullivanwriter
twitter.com/sullivan_writer
instagram.com/sullivan_writer

ACKNOWLEDGEMENTS

I want to thank my family and friends for all of their support. I want to thank all of my teachers who helped me become the writer I am today. I would also like to thank all of the authors who inspired me over the years and fueled my passion for telling stories.

Lastly, I would like to give a special thanks to Eric "Eagle Eyes" Dorflinger, Tod "The Typo God" Gamlen, and Christine "Copy Crusher" Flury. Their copyediting was as clutch as Howie Kendrick, who ended up smoking that pitch off of the foul pole, in case you didn't know.

Made in the USA
Coppell, TX
17 May 2020